Finding Insight

PRAISE FOR *FINDING INSIGHT*

"If there is insight about insight, *Finding Insight* delivers on that promise. Part insights cookbook, case study analysis, and research compendium, it was a refreshing read. Prepare to have your mind confronted, your practices challenged, and your sales growth supercharged. I'm glad I went along for the ride and hope to leverage these frameworks, tools, and hard-fought lessons in my own classroom and in my work with companies."

CHRISTINE MOORMAN, Founder, The CMO Survey and
T. Austin Finch Sr. Professor of Business Administration,
Fuqua School of Business, Duke University

"Marketing does not deliver ROI unless it changes human behavior, yet behavior change remains one of the most challenging tasks for the modern marketer. Behavior change requires deep human truth or real insight into why beliefs and behaviors exist. The authors of *Finding Insight* graciously suggests you don't need to read every page. I strongly suggest you read every word lest you find yourself settling for less than real insight and something far less than actual ROI."

DARYL TRAVIS, CEO, Brandtrust

"In my healthcare marketing career, I had the privilege of working directly with Mitch and Melinda. In reading *Finding Insight*, I am delighted by the way it captures the depth of their experience. Each chapter tells a story and shares a practical example. It reminds us and points out the importance of being curious, of listening, of learning and applying, thereby linking a business to its culture, its people and results. This is a valuable book. I will keep it close by!"

RICHARD D. PILNIK, chairman of the Board DiaMedica and
past president of Quintiles Commercial Solutions

"Insights is one of the most difficult topics to teach, and for many, difficult to even define. Mitch and Melinda have done a masterful job in demystifying this important topic and providing practical steps to find the insights that help your firm to create more value."

KEVIN McTIGUE, clinical professor of Marketing,
Kellogg School of Management

"*Finding Insight* is a must-read for marketers and market research. The biggest challenge that marketers face is making sense of the data they have. Sure, graphs and charts make it easier to see the data, but they often keep you from seeing the gold hidden in the data—that is the insights. These insights are not lying out in plain sight. Getting to the insights takes being curious, noticing what seems different than expected, and figuring out what to do with those details. What Spaulding and Tull have done in *Finding Insight* is lay out this problem, share why it happens, and then provide concrete and practical tools for solving the problem. Why I really love this book is that this skill is really hard to teach. It's easy to teach people how to make graphs. It's hard to teach them how to connect dots, dig deeper (a phrase my students are likely tired of hearing from me), sit with the data, and then go explore more information to really understand what's going on here. It's way easier for them to just create charts. I wish that I'd had *Finding Insight* for my students over the past twenty years. In addition, the repartee between Spaulding and Tull is fun to read. They have great examples, some of which I use in every class I teach. The combined skill and experience of these authors comes through in every chapter. I recommend anyone in business, but especially marketers who truly want to understand their customers, should read *Finding Insight*, and then practice using the ideas!"

M. KIM SAXTON, clinical professor of Marketing,
IU Kelley School of Business

"Back in 2001, as I transitioned into my first marketing leadership role, I was told by my mentor at the time that the key to understanding human behavior is to understand the unspoken truths behind those behaviors. And that the key to understanding those unspoken truths lies in one's ability to see beyond the obvious. The process of insights discovery and synthesis is undoubtedly the key to delivering truly differentiated marketing execution. It was through my work with Mitch and Melinda, which began decades ago, that my passion for cultivating this skillset was catalyzed. And this is where Mitch and Melinda excel in *Finding Insight*. Through a chapter story format, they bring to life how insights are discovered and, more importantly, how they drive impact when executed properly. For those who are seeking to deepen their skills on how best to navigate the process of getting to those unspoken truths that influence human behavior, *Finding Insight* provides a blueprint. Well done, Mitch and Melinda."

TONY EZELL, EVP, president North America &
chief marketing officer, Becton Dickinson

"I have been in the business of understanding human behavior in my customers, my employees, and my family for thirty-two years. I have discovered the most meaningful changes that I can help foster come from developing insights into the emotional experience of the people God sends to me. I am almost daily being asked to help find or unlock an insight to help a person overcome something terribly difficult. *Finding Insight* is an unbelievable tool for helping men like me. I so wish Melinda and Mitch had written this years ago. It will become a textbook for training leaders at Heart of a Man. The gateway to growth for every person is the insights that come from the help of a trusted friend. This is a powerful tool every leader needs to be competent in using."

BILL MOORE, CEO, Heart of a Man, and former CEO, PacMoore

"Insights-led marketing transformed my personal approach to marketing mid-career. I was taught by some of the brightest and best during what I consider to be my pivotal assignment of my marketing career, leading the Global Cialis team for over eight years. *Finding Insight* unlocks the power of insights and how to best leverage it for any brand. My first exposure was 2003, and twenty years later, the brand impact of this work remains though we're in a very different environment as marketers. The tactical implementation may have changed, the criticality to marketing strategy still burns brightly."

JOHN BAMFORTH, executive director, Eshelman Institute for Innovation, UNC Eshelman School of Pharmacy at Chapel Hill

"Melinda and Mitch's live learning programs have been a must for my team. I have seen the value of implementing their approach to insight development firsthand as a participant in their programs and as a leader in my organization. *Finding Insight* brings the essence of their live programs— how to connect the unconnectable—that is when the magic happens. For me personally, insight discovery is a part of human thinking that everyone has access to. Following their practical tips in this book will help anyone organize their thinking and confirm (or challenge) their gut feeling."

ETHEL LARSSON, vice president, head of Psychiatry Business Unit, Lundbeck U.S.

"To become a great marketer, you have to be able to discover and use insights. In *Finding Insight*, Mitch and Melinda share years of experience. They provide practical approaches from a mix of tools, techniques, and theories. This is also an entertaining resource, full of great examples and stories—ones in which the authors explain the key concepts, then provide questions to ask and the frameworks to use to move your brand or business forward."

TIM CALKINS, clinical professor of Marketing, Kellogg School of Management at Northwestern University

"Learn to Win has had the privilege of partnering with Mitch and Melinda for years, and their professionalism, humor, and insight into marketing capabilities have consistently impressed our team. *Finding Insight* offers a unique approach to understanding human behavior, helping to define and describe those deep truths that describe how people truly are. I highly recommend this book to anyone looking for a deeper understanding of the world around them and the people within it."

SASHA SEYMORE, co-founder & COO, Learn to Win

Discovering the
Non-Obvious Obvious Connection to
Why People Do What They Do

FINDING INSIGHT

Melinda Spaulding
Mitch Tull

NEW YORK

LONDON • NASHVILLE • MELBOURNE • VANCOUVER

Finding Insight

Discovering the Non-Obvious Obvious Connection to Why People Do What They Do

Published in New York, New York, by Morgan James Publishing. Morgan James is a trademark of Morgan James, LLC. www.MorganJamesPublishing.com

Proudly distributed by Publishers Group West®

Morgan James BOGO™

A **FREE** ebook edition is available for you or a friend with the purchase of this print book.

[_____]

CLEARLY SIGN YOUR NAME ABOVE

Instructions to claim your free ebook edition:
1. Visit MorganJamesBOGO.com
2. Sign your name CLEARLY in the space above
3. Complete the form and submit a photo of this entire page
4. You or your friend can download the ebook to your preferred device

ISBN 9781636983028 paperback
ISBN 9781636983035 ebook
Library of Congress Control Number: 2023949431

Cover & Interior Design by:
Christopher Kirk
www.GFSstudio.com

Morgan James is a proud partner of Habitat for Humanity Peninsula and Greater Williamsburg. Partners in building since 2006.

Get involved today! Visit: www.morgan-james-publishing.com/giving-back

To all those who want to improve their critical-thinking skills,
we humbly write this for you.

TABLE OF CONTENTS

WHY THIS BOOK? ACCORDING TO MELINDA

Mitch and I have taught insight discovery for our clients since 2015. We have provided learning programs on insights in a variety of formats, countries, and departments within our clients' organizations. Many people who have participated in our sessions have told us, "I learn something new every time I hear this." So I pondered, *Why are we continually asked to deliver this content?* I propose it's based on three primary reasons.

First, and probably most important, insights are foundational to building our relationships. As will be defined in the first chapter, an insight is a deep truth about a person or group of people that reaches the core of who they are and explains why they do what they do. I would argue the depth of any relationship is based on how well you know that person. Have you ever said someone knows you better than you know yourself? That person has an insight into you. I would wager that person also represents one of the closest, most cherished relationships in your life.

The next reason comes from one of Mitch's signature lines during our sessions: "Insights is one of the most abused and overused terms in our industry." This one stings a little bit for me because my industry—my colleagues—are guilty of this. I am guilty of this. I even used "insights" in my company name like so many other market research agencies. When technical words become colloquial, their true meaning can get lost. Mitch and I believe this has happened with *insights*. For this reason, we spend much of our time in our insights learning sessions defining an insight.

The last reason I believe we are repeatedly asked to share insights learning is that most of us have never been taught how to uncover insights—and this is my motivation for writing this book. Whether you are a marketer trying to uncover a deep truth about customers, a coach trying to motivate a team, a journalist trying to understand a subject, a politician trying to connect with constituents, or just a person trying to better understand another person, this book is for you.

WHY THIS BOOK? ACCORDING TO MITCH

The use of insights has been practiced in marketing since the 1960s and began primarily with the consumer packaged goods (CPG) industry. I was introduced to the term *insights* in 2003. I had been a business-to-business (B2B) brand marketer in the pharmaceutical industry for ten years. For an industry heavily focused on science and technology, the approach to marketing was product-centric, with communications revolving solely around the product's rational and functional benefits. It was also about this time when several disease areas were becoming more crowded with similar products that had only marginal differences. While this was a good thing for patients and physicians—more options equate to more choices—it was becoming increasingly difficult as a marketer to differentiate a brand for healthcare providers and patients based on the tangible benefits of the product alone.

I had just assumed a new leadership role in marketing training and development. Senior management had voiced their desire to move from a brand-centric to more of a human-insights-based approach. My team, along with other insight experts who had been recently hired by the company, was tasked with determining the capabilities, processes, methods, and learning programs needed to help marketers shift their mindsets and develop skills for how to achieve this goal. This was an enormous challenge, especially in an industry where everything revolved around science, innovation, and the product itself. Several questions surfaced as we began the journey of helping the organization move toward this new insights-based approach:

- Where should we start?
- Is there a standard definition and methodology for discovering and activating insights in business or academia that we can borrow from or adapt?
- What can we learn from business academia and successful organizations when it comes to building an insights-based capability?
- How do we equip marketers to recognize an insight from a fact, an observation, or an opinion?
- Should a brand focus on a single insight or many at a time?
- Who on a team decides whether the insight is a good one?
- Once we have an insight, how do we pull it through from strategy to execution so it does not get lost?
- What barriers will we need to overcome both at an individual and a company level to become more of an insights-based organization?
- What skills and competencies are required to excel at uncovering and activating insights?

As Melinda and I work with organizations today, we find ourselves continually asked these same questions. There have been a handful of books authored on the topic of insights with a primary focus on the "what" and "why." The goal of our book is to provide you with the "how" and the level of thinking you need to employ when it comes to the discovery and activation of an insight.

HOW TO READ THIS BOOK

We know people tend to skip around when reading business books. You, the reader, are likely to jump to the chapter that interests you the most or is most relevant to you now. We hope wherever you skip to, you find what you are looking for and enjoy it so much you go back and read the entire book—and suggest it as a "must-read" to your friends and colleagues.

Regardless of how you read this book, the following outline can help set expectations for the content. We have organized this book into three main sections.

1. An Overview of Insights
2. The 4 Pillars—Tools to Finding Insights
3. Connecting the Dots—Building Insight Capability and Competency

Each chapter of the three main sections has the following flow:

- A piece of comedy (You will learn why in Chapter 1)
- A personal story that reflects the content of the chapter
- The details of what we want you to know after reading the chapter
- A real-world example, typically about a product, since we are marketers
- A practice activity

As we say before every program we deliver, "Let's get started and have some fun!"

SECTION 1:

AN OVERVIEW OF INSIGHTS

A guy knows he's in love when he loses interest
in his car for a couple of days.
—Tim Allen, American comedian

"My Obsession with Mercedes Benz"—Mitch

When Melinda and I teach our introductory insights class, we typically start with a warm-up activity where we ask participants to write down their favorite brand. The usual responses (as one might predict) are Apple, Amazon, Costco, BMW, Netflix, and others like them. We then ask each participant to share why they chose their particular brand, and they usually tell some story behind their connection. As they speak about the brand, you can see their facial expressions becoming ones filled with delight and passion. When it comes to why they picked a certain brand, more of the answers given are based on how the product or service makes them feel versus the functional benefits it provides to them, which surprises many of the participants. At this point, we ask an additional question: "What do you believe this company or brand know about you?" This usually results in most admitting that it feels like the connection occurs because of the deep understanding the company has about their needs as a person. Once everyone has shared their story, someone will usually ask about Melinda's and my favorite brands. My answer is always Mercedes Benz.

My favorite brand story goes back to my dad's affection for cars. After his time in the Navy, he worked as a mechanic in the service department at the local GM dealership. Needless to say, every car he owned when my brother, sister, and I were growing up was a GM brand: Pontiac, Buick, Cadillac, Chevrolet, etc. So naturally, I also developed an affection for cars and drove a GM brand for several years until I became a brand manager for Eli Lilly and Company. I would travel to Europe and notice most taxis were Mercedes sedans. I asked a taxi driver one time why they all drove Mercedes. His response was, "Because they are luxurious and provide a comfortable ride for our passengers, but more importantly, they are sturdy and built to last."

When I received my first bonus as a manager, I decided it was time to make a trip to the local Mercedes dealership. After a couple of visits, I leased a C-280 sedan, which was their entry model at the time. I had been driving a Pontiac Grand Prix Special Edition. Believe me when I say, "There was nothing special about that car." It had several mechanical issues in the three years I had owned it. After signing the papers for the new Mercedes, my salesperson said I needed to make an appointment with the service manager. I found this puzzling. I asked why since I had just leased the car and it had less than twenty-five miles on the odometer. His reply was interesting. "It's what we require for every first-time Mercedes owner."

I remember going into the office to meet with Jerry, the service manager, who had worked for Mercedes for thirty years. Jerry welcomed me to the Mercedes Benz family and said, "Now that you have purchased your Mercedes, my job is to make sure we keep you in a Mercedes from now on. Although we don't have many mechanical issues with our cars, you will spend more time with me over the life of your Mercedes than with your salesperson." And then he turned to the window behind him. Through the window, across the street, was the Pontiac dealership where I had purchased my former car. Jerry pointed and said, "Let me tell you what your service experience has been like at that dealership."

He went on to describe an experience where your car needs repair. You call and schedule the appointment. You drive the car into the service bay in the morning. A young male (who may or may not have any mechanical experience) comes out to welcome you and inquires why you are bringing the car in for service. He will then ask if the car can be kept for the day. This necessitates a ride with someone to work. About mid-morning, you receive a call at work telling you they have discovered the problem, but they don't have the part, and it will need to be ordered, which could take a couple of days. He will also inform you the mechanic has also found something else that needs urgent attention and then try to upsell you to fix another issue you did not know was present. They finally call you on day three and say the car is ready to be picked up. You pick up the car, only to discover on the way home, the original problem has not been entirely fixed.

When Jerry finished, I thought to myself, "He knows exactly what I have experienced and has a deep understanding of the pain points I have encountered over the past three years."

Jerry then told me that his job and his service technicians' jobs were to make sure I never had that kind of experience with Mercedes. He described a different experience to me. When I bring the car in for service, I will be greeted by a seasoned service technician who has years of mechanical experience working on Mercedes vehicles and can diagnose my problem accurately. If the car needs to be kept for one day or a week, for whatever reason, I will be provided with a loaner vehicle at no charge, which eliminates the need to hitch a ride with someone to work. Once my car is serviced, it will be washed and vacuumed on the inside before pick-up.

Mercedes's customers can be described as accomplished, successful professionals/executives from elite industries or entrepreneurs. One of the core insights Mercedes is leveraging in their service experience for someone like me is that "time is money" for business professionals. In addition, executives like to feel "like executives," thus a Mercedes loaner is provided instead of a free rental car.

I can honestly say, after owning multiple Mercedes Benz vehicles over the past twenty-five years, I have never been disappointed. I will own a Mercedes until my wife or children take the keys. Mercedes Benz is just one example of a strong brand that understands the importance of connecting with its customers on both a functional and an emotional level to provide an exceptional customer experience—and this is an example of an insight in action!

Why Do Insights Matter?

The NINA Principle®: No Insight—No Advantage®
—Guiding mantra of Daryl Travis, founder and CEO, Brandtrust

When we teach insights, defining an insight is typically the second section of the agenda, not the first. Instead, as mentioned above in Mitch's story, we start with an activity we call "feeling the power of insights". We do this because starting with a definition can suggest insights are a formulaic activity rather than the underpinning foundation for a brand or company's strategy. It also allows participants to relate to what an insight feels like on a personal basis before analyzing them. Insights are more than words on the page; they are intuitive sentiments that connect with you or the people you care about at a deeper level. We need insights so we can more accurately see into situations to determine what action is required from us as marketers, service professionals, or just people who care about improving the experiences of others.

To borrow from a blog from the company Meeting Magic in the UK, "Insight is the bridge between the past and the future." We could not agree more. Most often, people are buried in information, and they struggle to make their way out of a data dump and into action. The intent of this book is to teach you the critical skills you need to process information into an insight that helps you take future action. Words like *transformative, disruptive*, and *innovative* are popular in the halls of organizations and the pitches of entrepreneurs—but what are these based on? We would argue strategies, even core values, should be based on insights. A marketer's job is to change behavior and create a future state. Analytics alone is based on examining past behavior data, whereas insights characterize the present state. Insights represent a deeper level of why we do what we do. If you want to change the future, you have to know where you are starting.

In this first section, we will provide a better understanding of insights at a definitional level, describe the common challenges to uncovering insights, and provide guidance on how to properly define problems to scope your insight discovery process. All of these pieces are fundamental to evolving from traditional summary and analysis to uncovering powerful insights.

CHAPTER 1:
WHAT IS AN INSIGHT?

It's so great to find that one special person
you want to annoy for the rest of your life.
—Rita Rudner, American comedian

"You Get Me"—Melinda

My husband and I had been married for just over two years. We purchased our first house and started a major renovation project. Therefore, it only seemed logical to dial back on how much we would spend at Christmas. We decided on a two-gift limit. We exchanged gifts right before we left for our road trip to see family. In the middle of the living room was something I had specifically asked for, a cedar chest to hold fabric for my sewing projects. I had a smile on my face when my husband said, "Open it."

I opened the lid, and my smile dropped with my reflexive eye roll. Inside the cedar chest was a box with a ribbon around it from a well-known lingerie shop. Before I could say anything, my husband said to me, "It's not what you think. Just open it."

With minimal enthusiasm, I opened the box to find what is one of the top five gifts I have ever received from Jeff, a plush navy blue bathrobe.

Even though I have now completely worn this bathrobe down to matted fibers, I keep it in a spare closet because of how much this gift means to me. This was a gift I did not ask for or even knew I wanted until I opened the box. It's meaningful because it is an example of how well my husband knows me—that he knew what I wanted before I did.

The bathrobe represents a deep truth about who I was at that time. I was working in a fairly stressful job that I absolutely loved. Trying to balance a new marriage, a new career, and a new home was a lot for me. The bathrobe was something I would not have purchased for myself. I prioritized things for the house, a special dinner out, a brief weekend trip with my husband, or clothes for work. I definitely did not prioritize something meant only for me and my comfort—and something that would never see the light of day. A bathrobe feels selfish when you have so many other priorities. My husband understood this about me, and that knowledge was the real gift. The bathrobe was just a symbol of his insight.

Insights Defined

If you've ever said to someone, "You get me" or thought to yourself, "That is so true; I never thought of that before," then you have experienced an insight. The formal definition we teach is an insight *is a deep truth that describes behavior* that is often unspoken. For example, a common generalization about wives and mothers is they often take care of everyone else's needs and wants before they take care of their own. In Melinda's story, her husband understood this about her. His combination of knowing this insight and finding something she would like but wouldn't prioritize for herself made the gift special. Gift-giving is a great example of insights in action. When a gift is the result of an insight into the recipient, the value is much greater than the purchase price.

In addition to giving or receiving a great gift, there are several other scenarios where you may have experienced an insight, such as:

1. A commercial that spoke directly to you and resulted in an emotional response, maybe even a purchase
2. A coach, teacher, or mentor who inspired you to improve when no one else could

3. A quote or phrase that connects with you enough to represent your identity—such that you use it in a signature line or even a tattoo

4. A comedian who made you laugh because they revealed the non-obvious obvious

Let's Get Emotional

Man is an emotional human being who describes things rationally. All behavior that we do, however, is actually governed by our emotions and feelings.
—Rob Malcolm, former CEO, Diageo

A question we are often asked is if insights must have an emotional component. Our answer is that most of the time, they do. In our experience, when insights don't have an emotional component, then it is not an insight. We encourage people to explore deeper to understand the *why* connected to the behavior. Let's take one of the most debated examples between the two of us. We like to call this insight "more dip on the chip."

Think back to the last time you shared a bowl of queso. Inevitably, someone was overly greedy with the queso, took more than the chip could handle, and a rogue chip became stuck in the dip, tainting the queso. Depending on how many were sharing the queso and how close you were to these people, the emotions likely ranged from a minor annoyance to significant disgust—and it ultimately suspended access to the dip for everyone. If you were the greedy offender, you had a dilemma on your hands. If only the host had splurged for the *Scoops*.

When we first shared "more dip on the chip" as an insight, we did not see it as having an emotional component. It was brought to our attention that the description above has emotions: greed, annoyance, and disgust. The emotions may seem silly or trivial but are there.

Insights can be big and provide understanding of harmful behaviors like smoking or maintaining toxic relationships—or they can be simple and recognize a pain point that may last only a few minutes. Small insights, like "more dip on the chip," might not solve a worldwide problem, but they are often harder to recognize because they are not top of mind.

Eureka! Ah-Ha! Well, Duh!!!

Think about a time you solved a difficult puzzle—such as a Wordle or a crossword puzzle that you mulled over much longer than you expected— or you finally determined how to enable technology you were struggling with (and perhaps even swearing at). You probably experienced a range of emotions. First, you felt a bit elated and accomplished, only to then feel somewhat deflated. The answer was probably simple but overlooked. Why hadn't you thought of it earlier?

Uncovering an insight is similar. When you uncover an insight, you have a "eureka" or "ah-ha moment." You feel a sense of accomplishment— until you share it with someone who says, "Well, duh."

Just like a puzzle or difficult problem, insights are often simple and have been there all along. For this reason, many insights experts, like Stan Sthanunathan, a former executive at Unilever, have described the uncovering of an insight as "retrospectively self-evident." The phrase addresses the response, "Well, duh. That seems obvious," and the question back should be, "*Yes, but was it obvious before I told you?*"

Insights are the non-obvious obvious. They are simple yet have deep meaning. When you hear an insight, you don't debate whether it is true or not. You already know it to be true; it just had not been brought to your attention before.

Who Are Insights for in the Real World?

Insights are relevant to a wide range of professional and personal situations. When we teach insights, we will often ask this question: Who is responsible for insights? The answer: Everyone. There is one notable profession, however, that is arguably the best at uncovering insights—comedians.

Great comedians are masters at observing our behavior, asking questions, and connecting the results of both to arrive at deep truths. Humor, at its best, is universal (even though it can be quite subjective) and requires the keenest of insights into the human experience. The comedic process requires a rigorous understanding of your subject, similar to that of an analyst. It is the product of non-linear thinking, usually using narrative and dialogue, to open minds to new ideas and seeing the world around them more clearly. Think of the last great stand-up bit you heard. Not the funniest one, but the *greatest* one. Our guess is it followed a formula. That is because, as Chris Rock said, comedians are "professional arguers. Not only can they argue about anything, but they can also argue either side." For jokes to ring true for many people, comedians must make a compelling case for their worldview. And they must do it in real time. Hours of preparation, research, trial and error, and, eventually, presentation go into the formulation of each joke and each performance. This process is nearly identical to anyone required to shape and present a point of view. So the next time you listen to a comedian and laugh out loud, pause and ask yourself if it is the result of an insight.

Several research studies explore how comedy and mood facilitate thinking. The two we find cited most frequently are from doctoral dissertations. The first, from Barry Kudrowitz—while studying at Massachusetts Institute of Technology (MIT)—found that improvisational comedians were more proficient at *idea generation* than professional product designers. The research further showed improvisational comedy training and activities can facilitate idea generation because they promote *associative thinking*.

You don't have to be a comedian to uncover insights. Just applying comedy to elevate someone's mood can be a tool to facilitate insightful thinking. Research conducted by Karuna Subramaniam, while at Northwestern University, evaluated the impact of mood on problem-solving. In the study, Subramaniam found that a positive mood facilitated increased problem-solving by participants compared to those in a less positive mood—especially problems that required creativity rather than analytics.

A Case for Associative Thinking

These days, many would argue nothing is truly new. Often, a new solution, innovation, or product is the combination of two or more existing concepts combined to solve a problem. Further, innovation is fleeting—because it must evolve.

Associative thinking is simply the practice of making connections between seemingly unrelated concepts and disciplines (combining existing knowns into something new). Throughout this book, the concept of associative thinking is present. It sounds simple but is necessary and perhaps the hardest part of insight discovery.

As Author Daniel Pink writes in his book, *A Whole New Mind*, "People who hope to thrive in the Conceptual Age must understand the connections between diverse, and seemingly separate, disciplines. They must know how to link apparently unconnected elements to create something new. And they must become adept at analogy—at seeing one thing in terms of another."

The case we outline for this chapter describes the result of associative thinking, which laid the foundation for the modern smartphone, forever changing the way we access global information today.

CASE: APPLE'S iPHONE—*"The One Device"*

Think back to the mobile phone you owned before 2007. It was probably a silver clamshell device with numeric keys on the bottom and a low-resolution screen on the top. It probably had a simple camera and a calendar and was capable of running a few basic games, but you used it primarily for voice calls and texting. The year 2007 is when Apple launched the iPhone—a device that would fundamentally transform how we interact with technology, culture, and each other.

"An iPod, a phone, and an internet communicator," Steve Jobs famously said on stage at Macworld in 2007 when unveiling the first iPhone. "Are you getting it? These are not three separate devices. This is one device." What seems natural today was frowned upon at the time. Few could imagine tapping on a small pane of glass instead of a hardware keyboard and using the smartphone as the main computer.

Some might argue 2007 became the pivotal year when we organized our communications experiences as before and after the iPhone.

Brian Merchant is a writer, editor, and producer whose work focuses on technology, climate, labor, and the stories we tell about the future. He is the author of *The One Device: The Secret History of the iPhone.* When the book hit bookstore shelves on June 20, 2017, it became a national best-seller. The *Wall Street Journal* called it "almost as addictive as the iPhone itself." Brian tells the untold account, ten years in the making, of the device that changed everything. Those who have read the book come away with a different appreciation for the level of associative thinking that was required by Apple's design engineers and the diverse and seemingly separate disciplines involved in the development of the iPhone. Looking back, people would say the idea of combining these three separate devices into one was a no-brainer—but it was not so at the time.

Perhaps the most interesting part of the story is that publicly, Jobs had been resistant to the idea of Apple making a phone. Before the iPhone, everyone at Apple thought cell phones "sucked." They were "terrible." Just "pieces of junk."

"Apple is best when it's fixing the things that people hate," said Greg Christie, who was head of Apple's Human Interface Group.

Mike Bell, a veteran of Apple, where he'd worked for fifteen years, and of Motorola's wireless division, was certain in his thinking that computers, music players, and cell phones were heading toward an inevitable convergence point. Merchant tells the story of how, on November 7, 2004, Bell sent Jobs a late-night email. "Steve, I know you don't want to do a phone," he wrote, "but here's why we should do it: Jony Ive has some really cool designs for future iPods that no one has seen. We ought to take one of those, put some Apple software around it, and make a phone out of it for ourselves instead of putting our stuff on other people's phones."

Jobs called him right away. They argued for hours, pushing back and forth. Bell detailed his convergence theory—no doubt mentioning that the mobile phone market was exploding worldwide—and Jobs picked it apart. But finally, he relented.

"Okay, I think we should go do it," he said. Bell, Jobs, and Ive had lunch three or four days later and kicked off the iPhone project—and the rest is history.

The iPhone is a real-world example of associative thinking, allowing users to get all of their needs accomplished in one device. It is also an example of how barriers exist to insight discovery. Steve Jobs didn't want to launch a phone. Yet it seems he hired smart people and entertained different ideas and perspectives. Even if it took hours of arguing and debate, Steve Jobs acquiesced, and the development kicked off within weeks. Insight discovery is hard because it is unnatural for us to seek out others with different ideas. We like confirmation rather than debate.

This is only a sneak peek into associative thinking, so we will return to this topic in the final section of this book, which covers synthesis—how to connect the data and tools to arrive at and refine our insights.

In our next chapter, we will dive deeper into details about the challenges and barriers to insight discovery.

Practice: Feel the Power of an Insight

Write down your favorite brand. This is a brand you hold in high regard, use regularly, and/or depend on.

- Why did you select this brand?
- How does your experience with this brand make you feel when you are consuming or interacting with it?
- How are consumers of this brand different from those that do not consume this brand?
- Think about someone giving you this brand as a gift (similar to Melinda's story). What did the person know about you to determine it would be a good gift?

CHAPTER 2:
WHY ARE INSIGHTS SO HARD TO FIND?

Never underestimate the power of stupid people in large groups.
—George Carlin, American comedian

"Moving Beyond Stereotypes"—Mitch

I grew up in Tull, Arkansas, a small southern rural city, with a population of 500 and named after my ancestors. From that description, you might imagine I have a Southern accent. Moving to the Midwest to work for a large pharmaceutical company, it quickly became apparent there were associations and perceptions placed on me when I spoke. He must be friendly, social, fun . . . but not necessarily the "sharpest tool in the shed," as we say in the South. It occurs less often today, but it was not too many years ago that people from the South were stereotyped and labeled as "rednecks" or "hillbillies" and perceived to be backward, simple, unsophisticated, slow-talking, and less educated than those in the northern states.

I had been a sales representative for a large global pharmaceutical company in Arkansas for five years. I had great success at it and consistently ranked in the top 10 percent in sales performance among my peers year after year. Management was considering me for a corporate position in the global headquarters. This was a big deal, as it was the path to move up in the company. Once I was placed on a list for consideration, my manager had a frank conversation with me based on feedback from his boss. I needed to drop the Southern colloquialisms. They were both concerned about how I would be perceived—and, of course, how they would be perceived—working in a global corporate environment. This may be surprising in today's world, but according to a study by the University of Chicago and the University of Munich, people with a Southern accent could lose out on thousands of dollars per year. The research revealed that people with strong regional accents face a wage penalty of up to 20 percent, compared to those who speak with a "standard accent."

Despite my boss and his boss's advice, I refused to alter my accent and had to work hard when I first encountered someone new to overcome the stereotype and label placed on me by some. On the flip side, I worked the last twelve years of my corporate career as head of the global marketing training and development group. The job afforded me the ability to work and travel with a variety of people from different cultures and from over thirty different countries. This was a great learning experience, as it allowed me to overcome some of the stereotypes, labels, and perceptions I had falsely attributed to various cultures and people who were different from me.

Today, when Melinda and I present to groups, I call out my accent upfront and joke that Melinda will translate my Southern phrases. My Southern roots and accent are core to who I am—always have been and will continue to be—and have played a big role in why I am successful today.

I started my career as a pharmacist. When you are a pharmacist in rural Arkansas, you have to get to know a wide range of people. You must interpret phrases like, "I think my sugars are runnin' high" to understand *I have not been compliant with my diabetes medication*. Perhaps it gives me an edge when it comes to insights because I can cut through corporate speak, seek to understand others, and get to the heart of the matter by keeping things simple. I guess this phrase is true: "You can take the boy out of the country, but you can't take the country out of the boy."

We Make Things Up

There are many reasons insights are hard to uncover. The biggest, we would argue, is that we live on false beliefs. To quote the sociologist Howard Becker, "In the absence of real knowledge, our imagination takes over. We impute points of view, perspectives, and motives to the people we study." We give embedded meaning to things without our awareness.

We make things up and tend to do it in both our personal and professional lives, but why? First and foremost, it's efficient—breaking down fiction or obtaining a deeper understanding of someone else takes time. For example, think about the last time you flew on a Southwest Airlines flight where there was open seating (first come, first served). One does not have the time to get to know the people before deciding to sit next to them on the flight. So we pick a seat next to someone based on outward appearance, hygiene, children versus no children, and other judgments because there is no time to understand who they really are before making our selection.

Second, we make things up to make sense of the world. Our natural way of processing new information is to fit it into our pre-established models and beliefs. It is the way language works, how we name things. We forget these models and beliefs are always limited because they are merely a representation of our reality and not reality itself.

A third reason is the media and the digital world have a huge influence and greatly contribute to shaping our images, impressions, and stereotypes of others. We live in an age today where we want instant answers and are quick to "google" or search the internet for information, often leading us to biased sources that may not reflect reality or the truth. Behind every internet search engine is a set of instructions called an *algorithm* that determines which results best match your query and in what order they should appear. These algorithms reflect the implicit or explicit biases of the people who program them. In addition, social media has become a major force in shaping politics, business, world culture, education, careers, innovation, and more. The echo chamber effect of social media occurs when harmonious people unite and develop tunnel vision. Participants in online discussions may find their opinions constantly echoed back to them, which reinforces their individual belief systems because of the declining exposure to others' opinions.

Fourth, we work with simplified data that lacks context. Today, there are entire departments within organizations focused on data analytics using advanced sources of data collection for analysis, such as artificial intelligence, machine learning, text analytics, social media listening, predictive analytics, and more, without ever talking directly to a human being. The challenge with these new forms of data when it comes to finding insights is they tend to be more observational and based on model assumptions. Often, a body of data can create an image or picture of a situation, a person, or a customer, but it does not provide the full texture and context of *why* the behavior is occurring, so our imaginations or the machines fill that in.

It is not to be intentionally biased, but our brains have created shortcuts without our awareness. These shortcuts can be equally helpful and dangerous at the same time. For this reason, our first barriers to insight discovery are *personal bias, stereotypes, and mental shortcuts.*

Other Common Barriers to Finding Insights

Mental Fixation

The first phase of an Aha! experience requires the problem solver to come upon an impasse, a place where they become stuck, and even though they believe they have explored all the possibilities, they are still unable to retrieve or generate a solution. Some research suggests that insight problems are difficult to solve because of our mental fixation on the inappropriate aspects of the problem content. We focus on the problem rather than the person. In addition, people can get trapped by the initial framing of the problem, according to the author of *What's Your Problem?*, Thomas Wedell-Wedellsborg. Insight is believed to occur with a break in this mental fixation. Wedellsborg suggests overcoming this trap by reframing the problem. Looking at the problem from different angles often makes new connections more obvious.

Ignoring Habits

Social psychologists estimate that 45 percent of our daily behavior is habitual. Habits are our brain's default option and influence a wide range of highly complex behaviors. In Charles Duhigg's *New York Times* best-seller, *The Power of Habits*, he says, "Habits shape our lives far more than we realize—they are so strong, in fact, that they cause our brains to cling to them at the exclusion of all else, including common sense." They are so deeply embedded in our subconscious that we are often unaware of them in our daily routines. Often, when people are being interviewed in a research setting about a topic, they will provide a rational answer or what they perceive to be the correct answer. However, if you were to follow and observe their behavior outside of the research setting, their behavior would not align with what they stated they were doing. Some might accuse them of being dishonest.

We would say it is likely a habit is at play in their subconscious, and the individual is unaware it is driving their behavior.

The challenge when we are looking for insights is that we ignore these habits when attempting to understand the *why* behind someone else's behavior. This results in failing to see the full picture. Companies spend billions to advertise their messages to us, relying on us to remember their brands, slogans, claims, and prices, but our memories are remarkably unreliable; as a result, much of their advertising dollars are wasted. Duhigg suggests that deconstructing the habit of an individual to understand the trigger or cue that initiates their routine and the associated reward for the behavior is more likely to result in seeing more of the whole picture, and therefore, allows us to see the connections that might uncover a potential new insight.

Groupthink

The path to insights is hard enough. Facts, understandings, and insights don't come packaged in obvious ways. An unrecognized barrier, which makes it even harder for many, is that we have accepted certain "truths," based on the groups and teams we are a part of in our personal and business lives. Teams or organizations that have been together over time or a strong member of the team can create internal momentum around a false view of a situation or customer. As a result, momentum builds on beliefs that aren't grounded in reality. The momentum often takes over, and anything that doesn't fit is considered an outlier.

Have you ever experienced someone on the team or someone in management having a particular bias that rules all decisions? How frustrating it can be when the facts you collect don't confirm that bias. A critical aspect for overcoming this subtle barrier is to ensure there is cognitive diversity, with different brains around the table possessing conflicting opinions with different sets of experiences. As difficult as it may sound, vigorous debate, discussion, consideration, investigation, and resolve can take time but is a necessary part of the insight process in reducing groupthink and overcoming a team's blind spots.

A Desire for Perfection and Predictability

Insight is the opposite of predictability. Insights are disruptive. They come without warning, take unexpected forms, and open unimagined opportunities. Gary Klein is a research psychologist famous for pioneering the field of naturalistic decision-making. In his book, *Seeing What Others Don't,* he dedicates an entire chapter to how organizations inadvertently suppress the insights of their workers and do so in ways that are ingrained and invisible. He argues, "Organizations stifle insights because of forces locked deep inside their DNA: they value predictability, they recoil from surprises, and they crave perfection, the absence of errors."

Executives may believe they want insights and innovations but are most receptive to new ideas that fit within existing practices and maintain predictability. At an individual level, we don't like to rethink our decisions and are resistant to change. In working with organizations, we will often hear people say things like, "Your idea is interesting, but that's not the way we do it here" or "There are too many unknowns and uncertainties; plus we don't know what the ROI will be," or even, "It is too risky, and nobody is willing to take responsibility if it fails." In addition, organizations naturally gravitate toward reducing errors, which seems pretty straightforward. However, insights can take us beyond perfection. They can show us ways to improve or change the original plan if we are willing to let go of existing practices and stop striving for perfection.

Over-Reliance on Process and Schedules

Any well-run organization or team incorporates processes, procedures, schedules, checklists, and timelines for efficiency purposes. It is a necessary discipline. However, the challenge, when it comes to finding insights, is that the discovery process is not linear or time-bound. Every year, organizations and teams go through a business planning cycle, and many start by looking at existing and/or new insights to start the process. We like to remind teams that insight discovery and generation do not live on a fixed timeline or schedule that stops and starts with annual business planning. Insights can surface at any time, and usually, they emerge when least expected. In addition, the number of reviews by various functions and people (especially in large organizations) required throughout the planning process can work against insight discovery by either diluting or stifling a potential new insight through consensus decision-making.

A Lack of Training

Arriving at a clear and powerful insight is harder than it seems. It doesn't have to be. It can be learned, taught, and mastered. Most people have never had any formal training or education when it comes to how to uncover an insight and, instead, rely solely on their market research or creative agencies to do the work. Brandtrust founder and CEO, Daryl Travis, in his book *How Does It Make You Feel?*, points out that most business schools do not teach the emotional side of branding, which is a poor state of affairs. So, unless people have worked for a Proctor & Gamble, Coke, or another consumer packaged goods company, where insight training is an integral part of their educational development, they most likely have never learned or been formerly taught what an insight is or how to uncover a good one. Our experience in the B2B healthcare industry is that often what are being called insights are nothing more than facts, summaries of the obvious, or biased opinions, which tend to be subjective and superficial. As you will read in the next section of this book, finding insights is not formulaic, but there are methodologies and tools that can be learned and applied to aid in your insight discovery efforts.

Summary of Common Barriers to Look Out For

Barrier	Observations to Suggest This Barrier Exists
Personal Bias / Stereotypes / Mental Shortcuts	• No evidence for the *why* behind behavior • "Facts" are described rather than sourced • Reluctance to seek confirmation or a different opinion
Mental Fixation	• Multiple meetings with no concrete next steps • A single or few data points are consistently mentioned as the source of a problem
Ignoring Habits	• Frustration that customers say one thing and do another—a belief they are "lying to us" • Customers struggle to describe their behavior or reasons for their behavior
Groupthink	• Ignoring or dismissing data that does not support the accepted conclusion • Unwillingness to try new research techniques or gather new data/perspectives
A Desire for Perfection and Predictability	• Phrases like, "That's too risky" or "We can't do that because we have never done it before" • Repeating the same fact-finding research to confirm assumptions
Over-Reliance on Process and Schedules	• Timelines dictate the research or learning plans more so than the objectives • Delaying the socialization of research findings/insights because the brand plan is too far along, and it will challenge the strategy
A Lack of Training	• The term *insights* is overused in meetings and presentations with inconsistent meaning • Facts, summaries, and conclusions are all considered insights • A team's insights are a laundry list rather than a condensed set of a few statements

Be Curious, Not Judgmental

When we teach our insight discovery classes, we stress that one of the key traits necessary in the exploration and discovery of insights is to be curious and ask a lot of *why* questions—especially when it comes to problem definition. In clearly defining a problem, one needs to look at a situation from multiple angles and perspectives and look beyond the obvious to see the non-obvious.

Curiosity is defined as a state of active interest or genuinely wanting to know more about something. It allows us to embrace unfamiliar circumstances, giving us a greater opportunity to experience discovery and joy. Indeed, studies show that life is better when we are curious. People are better at learning information they are curious about, as curiosity prepares the brain for learning and makes subsequent learning more enjoyable and rewarding.

Both of us read *Curious George* to our kids when they were younger. George is a fictional monkey with no tail and was described as very curious—always asking, "Why?" He celebrates the curiosity, creativity, and pure joy that comes with the innocence of childhood. Unfortunately, we all lose that child-like curiosity somewhere along the way to becoming adults.

Think about when you were a young child and first started coloring. You would proudly bring a page out of your coloring book to your parents or kindergarten teacher. It was probably hard to discern what the picture was supposed to resemble because you colored outside the lines. You were celebrated and praised for what a good job you had done on your unrecognizable picture. As you grew older and went off to grade school, you became conditioned to color inside the lines. With boundaries and more accumulation of knowledge, you unintentionally but slowly lost your curiosity and creativity.

So we encourage our teams to be "like Curious George" and have a beginner's mind, driving them to explain the unexpected and resolve uncertainty. This requires being open and not emotionally connected to the problem at hand, asking lots of "I wish I knew" questions for greater learning, welcoming new information and perspectives, and not assuming anything. Sounds easy but it is hard to do in real life.

We live in a world today that is on information overload. Cassini Nazir, an assistant professor at the College of Visual Arts and Design at the University of North Texas, says, "Hidden inside that information are our deeply held beliefs which give us firm notions about other people, situations, products, etc. We tend to make up our minds too quickly, holding onto ideas that may be incomplete, inaccurate, wrong, and sometimes harmful. And the worst part is, we don't even realize it. The more firmly we hold on to our notions, the greater the illusion that we possess knowledge. So, to avoid these notions, we must seek out curiosity."

As mentioned earlier, groupthink can unknowingly stifle curiosity. Often, the amount of cognitive diversity and the makeup of teams has a direct bearing on the level of curiosity being employed at any given time. We encourage experienced teams to consider inviting others to join who are not as close to the problem or who are new to the category. The new person will be more eager to learn and will usually have many questions, which the team may have ignored, assumed were unimportant, or need to revisit. I know it sounds counter-intuitive, but the less knowledgeable members of a team can serve as catalysts for looking at a problem in new and fresh ways.

Intelligent ≠ Insightful

A common misconception is that insight is directly related to intelligence. Actually, intelligence can be another barrier to insight discovery. Organizational psychologist and popular science author Adam Grant, who wrote *Think Again,* includes a section called "The Smarter They Are, The Harder They Fail." In this section, he shares research findings that the higher someone's IQ, the more likely they are to fall for stereotypes and struggle to update their beliefs. Being intelligent—and knowing it—means you have a blind spot to accepting another point of view. He further shares research that shows analysts are best when looking at neutral data. However, when the data being analyzed has a strong emotional connection or relates to a personal ideology, such as a political issue, the analyst's skills become a liability. As he concludes, "The better you are at crunching numbers, the more spectacular you fail at analyzing patterns that contradict your views."

Does this mean insights are only for the average or below-average intelligent person? Of course not. Instead, it means we must be cautious of our "expert opinions." The stronger we believe we are right about something, the more likely we need to be open to challenges from someone who we believe is wrong.

Back when education first used the term *gifted* to describe intelligence, a paper was published that hypothesized "insight" was a dimension missing from the IQ construct. The authors proposed to add insight as a sub-theory to measure intelligence with the following as their reason: "Significant and exceptional intellectual accomplishment (such as a major scientific discovery) almost always involves major intellectual insights. The thinker's gifts seem directly to lie in their insight abilities and abilities to do non-entrenched thinking, rather than in their IQ-like abilities or their mere abilities to process information rapidly." This is another reason insight discovery is a practice for more than marketing and marketing research professionals.

Hopefully, you are concluding that 1) insights are important and 2) insights are difficult to uncover. If not, we are, of course, open to an alternative point of view. If you are still with us on these two conclusions, then read the following classic case of a real-world example of how the "experts" got it wrong.

CASE: COKE—*"Even the Best Get it Wrong"*

Coca-Cola is perhaps one of the most valuable brands in the world. Further, it is a company whose leaders have invested heavily in insight discovery—in fact, they set up the endowment for the graduate program in market research at the University of Georgia. So how could they get it so wrong with New Coke? Those of you who remember the '80s know the New Coke story. There are multiple articles, business cases, chapters in textbooks—even a dedicated section on the Coca-Cola website called "The Story of One of the Most Memorable Marketing Blunders Ever." For the rest of you, here is a brief synopsis.

Coca-Cola has dominated the cola wars for decades, but not without significant competition from Pepsi. The battle between these two brands is a classic example of a leader and a challenger. Perhaps it is fitting that the Pepsi Challenge was the campaign that put the executives at Coke most on the defensive.

The Pepsi Challenge consisted of blind taste tests where consumers took a sip of two colas—one was Coke and one was Pepsi. After the participants selected the soda they preferred, the stats proved that, more often, Pepsi was favored. The television commercials started with customers stating how much they *didn't like* Pepsi, only to reveal from the blind test, they had selected it over Coke.

The Pepsi Challenge campaign was successful, as evidenced by an increase in market share at the cost of Coca-Cola. Why did consumers select Pepsi over Coke? The answer was simple. Pepsi is sweeter than Coke. The executives at Coca-Cola knew this and, in response, altered their secret formula to increase the sweetness of the cola. Extensive market research was conducted. Almost 200,000 blind taste tests led to the same conclusion; the new formula of Coke would win in taste tests, even among the most loyal Pepsi drinkers.

As then Coca-Cola President Donald Keough would say, "I've never been as confident about a decision as I am about the one we're announcing today." What was that announcement? A product called New Coke would replace Coca-Cola—not an additional option, but a complete replacement. Consumers were outraged. Coca-Cola was flooded with calls. Consumers held protests. Some stockpiled as much of the original Coca-Cola as they could find in their basements. After seventy-nine days, the original Coke was placed back on the market with a new addition to their label: "classic." Quickly, the classic cola regained its market share, if not rising higher than before.

How could almost 200,000 taste tests be wrong? The marketing debate ranges from strategy to picking apart the challenges with the "blind" taste test. We will add our theory into the mix: pick any of the barriers we outlined above. What all barriers we mentioned have in common is that of a myopic view. Biases, groupthink, desire for perfection . . . they all highlight a core human insight about ourselves: we don't like conflicting information. The executives at Coca-Cola didn't ask the fundamental question, which was, "Even though you like this new cola over the others, how would you feel if it replaced the Coca-Cola you know?"

Some hypothesize the marketing executives at Coke concocted this plan all along to regain consumer loyalty. It was all a big stunt that, in the end, paid off. Publicly, Keough said, "The truth is we're not that dumb, and we're not that smart." Being true to our prior section, we must be open to that possibility.

The case of New Coke underscores the importance of something we like to call "cognitive diversity." We would propose the team at Coke likely would not entertain failure for their New Coke plan. It had to work. They felt the heat of competition and needed to act as fast as possible. Hearing an opposing view to their plan created a new, even greater problem. That they did not have a solution to the Pepsi Challenge. They would have to go back to the drawing board, despite the effort and expense thrown at New Coke.

Even though it goes against our nature, in insight discovery, it is important to seek people who think differently from us. Debate is good. Conflicting ideas are critical. Insight discovery is not about right or wrong. It is about asking tough questions like, "Who would disagree with us and why? How can I prove my assumptions are wrong?" Imagine if the team at

Coke had conducted unblinded as well as blinded taste tests. We hypothesize the results would be very different. If that were true, what would they have learned about their consumers? Perhaps that a cola, for many, wasn't *just* a cola. It is a statement about the consumer. Like being a Democrat or a Republican, people classify themselves as a Coke or a Pepsi drinker.

This case has had applications for a variety of business frameworks. We placed it here, assuming half of our readers would remember the New Coke phenomenon and the other half will have heard about it from marketing textbooks or documentaries like "Pepsi, Where's My Jet?" Regardless of its application, it underscores the difficulty of insight discovery. We have assumptions and biases that prevent us from seeing the big picture. Often these barriers are present from the beginning of the insight discovery process in a step we refer to as "problem definition."

The next chapter is intended to start your insight discovery in the right direction by ensuring you are defining the correct problem. In the Coke case, the executives anchored their problem in the taste test. Their assumption was beating the taste test would solve their market share decline to Pepsi. They set off to solve the problem of developing a drink to beat Pepsi in a blind taste test. That proved to be the wrong problem. As you read the next section, be thinking about when problem definition was the culprit for a challenge you experienced.

Practice: Source of Bias

Write down the name of a celebrity or another public figure, someone you recognize but do not know personally. Next, write down five adjectives you would use to describe this person. Next to each adjective, write down your source for that adjective.

Now that you have done this, reflect on your sources. Which adjective are you most certain is correct? Which one are you most uncertain about? The point of this exercise is not to be right or wrong but to uncover sources of bias. We are all biased. We can never become unbiased, but we can become aware of our biases. Knowing our blind spots can help us identify when we need to check our facts or reach out to someone with a different perspective.

CHAPTER 3:
SO WHAT'S YOUR PROBLEM?

You know there is a problem with the education system
when you realize that out of the 3 Rs, only one begins with an R.
—Dennis Miller, American comedian and commentator

"Underestimating the Problem"—Mitch

It was the summer of 2000. I had been a brand marketer in diabetes for seven years and had successfully helped launch two important products globally for Eli Lilly and Company: Humalog, the first rapid-acting insulin analog, and Actos, an oral insulin sensitizer. This combined with five years as part of the hospital sales division was seen as an ideal combination to tackle the next launch. Lilly had been working on developing a treatment for severe sepsis for nearly twenty years. Efforts finally yielded positive results with the development of Xigris, also called "activated protein C." It was a genetically engineered version of the human-activated protein C molecule that occurs naturally in the blood and, at the time, was one of the most complex biotechnology products ever developed.

Sepsis is a major cause of death. With our market analysis, we knew about 750,000 people develop sepsis each year in the United States, of whom approximately 225,000 die as a result (i.e., a mortality rate of about 29 percent). Although the incidence of sepsis is relatively small compared to other medical conditions, a significant percentage of patients who die from severe sepsis do so within a week of contracting the disease.

Severe sepsis occurs most often in patients in intensive care units (ICUs), those already being treated for trauma, surgery, burns, cancer, or pneumonia. ICUs are advanced and highly specialized units within hospitals. These units provide care to medical or surgical patients whose conditions are life-threatening and require comprehensive care and constant monitoring.

Lilly had conducted a global Phase III clinical trial for Xigris, and study results were so positive that, as dictated by the test protocol, Lilly ended the study eighteen months ahead of schedule. Typically, a new drug in development is required to show positive results in two well-controlled clinical Phase III trials. However, because of the lack of effective treatments and the extremely high mortality rates for sepsis, the FDA was willing to accept the results of one positive trial for ethical reasons for submission and consideration for approval. Needless to say, the senior leadership team at Lilly was very enthusiastic about the potential for Xigris; it was one of the top priorities of the company. I was offered and accepted the opportunity to become part of the Xigris launch team. I was excited to be part of introducing new, lifesaving technology that worked for these patients.

Expectations were high in the first year of the launch. The drug was unique and saved lives, giving Lilly an opportunity to set a high price in an effort to recoup the hundreds of millions of dollars the company had invested in research and testing. The promotion plans seemed clear, with a focus on communicating the core benefit of Xigris: reduced mortality. Reaching critical care specialists, such as critical care pulmonary professionals and anesthesiologists, was important but so was reaching pharmacists, insurance company policymakers, and hospital administrators, who would all play a role in the decision to use Xigris. With an initial price of $6,800 for a four-day course of therapy in the ICU, based on cost-effectiveness studies, Xigris would be one of the most expensive drugs a hospital would carry at the time. There were few comparable drugs in the market. Because of concerns about healthcare costs, there was a risk that the use of such an expensive drug would be restricted by private insurance companies, Medicare, Medicaid, and hospitals.

Securing approval from the US Food and Drug Administration (FDA) to market Xigris was far more challenging than our team had anticipated. Following standard procedures for evaluating a new drug, the FDA created an advisory board panel to review the Xigris submission. The review did not go smoothly. The panel noted that Xigris did not appear to work as well in patients with less serious forms of sepsis. The panel also expressed concerns about the risk of serious internal bleeding. The final result was a 10-10 split among the panel members, and this caused a tremendous amount of skepticism among all those involved. The academic community moved from lamenting no successful sepsis drugs to cynicism/criticism mode. The FDA would go on to approve Xigris for adult patients with severe sepsis with a high risk of death. The FDA noted that it should not be used for patients with a number of specific medical problems, such as stroke and head trauma.

Lives were saved with the approval of Xigris, but despite the company's best efforts, the launch did not meet its financial objectives with sales goals in the first year. It was frustrating and disappointing to have a product that saved lives but never met its true expectations over time. How could this have happened? People within the company and external key opinion leaders had assumed, because Xigris was a breakthrough technology, it would be successful. Some key opinion leaders even commented when they first saw the clinical data, "This product is going to sell itself."

Another false hypothesis was that those who worked in the ICU knew how to readily identify patients with severe sepsis and would know when to use Xigris. However, there was no clear consensus or universal guidelines at the time to treat severe sepsis among critical care specialists and professional associations, so education became critically important and time-consuming. In addition, physicians could not determine precisely when to use the product—and this was a major problem. This resulted in only the most severe patients receiving Xigris too late in the disease progression to make a difference.

Some of the insights that were missed or overlooked included that the need for speed is real in the ICU. With their treatments and procedures, ICU physicians were used to real-time feedback and instant gratification. All the medications they used in the ICU before Xigris could be measured at the bedside. With Xigris, a bag of clear liquid was administered for four days. However, there was no consistent real-time feedback for physicians to know if it was working until days later. Xigris had shown statistical significance in reducing mortality across many patients in the Phase III clinical trial. However, at an average-sized hospital, if Xigris was used on all patients with severe sepsis (which accounted for only 10 percent of ICU patients at any one time), only one patient a month would be saved. It could take four months on average for an individual ICU physician to experience having one patient saved by Xigris.

We were so focused on the solution that we underestimated the complexity of the business challenge and the problems faced in pioneering a new category. There are few norms to follow when you are first and people are reluctant to change and wary of risks. Establishing new behaviors is difficult without clearly understanding the underlying needs and deep insights about those who are involved in the decision to use the product.

In my career, I have launched three major pharmaceutical products. Two were successful. Despite the lackluster performance of Xigris relative to the others, it is probably the experience I learned from the most.

Problem Definition First

When we first started facilitating our traditional learning programs on insights, they did not include problem definition. We saved this topic for Market Research Design and How to Be a Better Strategic Consultant. As our work with clients progressed, we realized the importance of bringing problem definition into insight discovery. When we don't accurately understand or define the true problem from the start, we are sent down the wrong path for a solution and gather the wrong information. Like the Xigris example, we get caught up in the opportunity and the solution we can offer without recognizing the real problem, its challenges, and the underlying needs associated with it. For this reason, we feel strongly that proper problem definition is a critical tool and should be the starting point for insight discovery.

What Is the Problem to Be Solved?

Talk to anyone who solves other people's problems, and you will find most start by asking, "What problem are you trying to solve?"

Human-centered design is an approach to problem-solving that focuses on customers' underlying needs. Needs are unsatisfied actions, behaviors, or beliefs that arise from an unsolved problem, which often remains unnoticed, undiagnosed, or unarticulated.

In the 1960s, Jacob Getzels, a famous educator and one of the founders of creativity research at the University of Chicago, recognized the importance of defining the right problem, not just seeking the right solution. In school, problems tend to be presented in a nice orderly manner. Mihaly Csikszentmihalyi, one of Getzels's protégés and co-authors, said, "[In] Most schools, all you learn is solving problems; then you get out in the real world, [and] you feel lost because nobody's telling you what problem to solve. In real life, most of us are not confronted with clearly stated problems with a simple solution. Usually, we must first say what the problem is."

Getzels wrote that problems with complex matters typically appear in three forms:

Problem Type 1: An ill-defined mess or pain point

Often, the cause of the pain is unclear. Pain points cause people to jump to solutions without pausing to consider what's going on. Examples:

- We are not meeting our sales goals. *Therefore, we need to change our positioning and messaging for the brand*
- Surveys show that 50 percent of our staff do not want to return to the office post-COVID. *Therefore, we need to offer more incentives to make people want to return to the office*

Problem Type 2: A goal we don't know how to reach

When facing a pain point, you at least know where to start. For goals, you have a defined ending but maybe not a defined beginning. Examples:

- Have enough COVID-19 vaccine for all people in the United States who wish to be vaccinated
- Motivate flu sufferers to seek treatment within their first forty-eight hours of symptoms

Problem Type 3: Someone fell in love with a solution

Sometimes people fall in love with an idea with zero to minimal evidence that the solution solves a real-world problem. The solution is often disguised as a problem. Examples:

- We need to develop better education to promote healthier eating through the use of a mobile app
- We are experiencing an increasing number of employees leaving because salaries are below the industry's average

Problem Definition Is an Iterative Process

Organizations often reward productivity and the completion of projects. As a result, marketing and market research often start with a research plan rather than defining the specific problem. We, as marketers and researchers, must spend the time to define the problem and capture the information we need to inform our decisions. We find teams, more often than not, rush the process and assume our customers can give us the answer.

Author and expert in problem-solving Thomas Wedell-Wedellsborg suggests in his book *What's Your Problem?* the process should start with creating a short problem statement by writing the problem down as a complete sentence. There are many benefits to writing down your problem, such as slowing things down to prevent people from jumping into solution mode. It also forces you to be specific and makes it easier to look objectively at a problem. It need not be a perfect description of the issue but can serve as an anchor for discussion. We find most people and teams struggle in writing a problem statement. Often, there is a lack of true understanding of the situation and many questions go unanswered, something we call "I wish I knews" (IWIKs). We suggest a six-step framework that has been helpful for us in working with others to help ensure a problem is clearly defined.

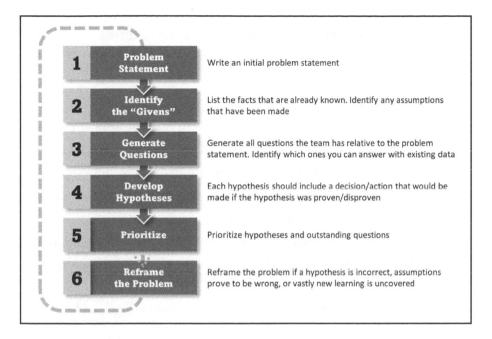

Step 1: Write a Problem Statement

A good problem statement clarifies the current situation by specifically identifying the problem and its severity, location, and financial impact. It also serves as a great communication tool, helping to get buy-in and support from others. When problem statements are well written, people readily grasp and understand what you are trying to accomplish.

This might sound obvious, but write the problem statement with the audience in mind. You will most likely have to convince a board or some other governing body to provide resources to solve the problem and enlist team members to assist you. You do not want to spend your precious time explaining over and over what you are trying to accomplish.

A problem statement should be concise and include:

- A brief description of the problem and the metric used to describe the problem
- Where the problem is occurring by name and location

- The time frame over which the problem has occurred
- The size or magnitude of the problem

You must be careful to avoid underwriting a problem statement. A natural tendency is to write a problem statement too simplistically because you are already familiar with the problem. If you are going to recruit support and resources to solve your problem, others have to understand the context and the significance to support the task force or team assigned to develop and/or deliver the proposed plan.

A poor problem statement is followed by an example of an acceptable problem statement. First up, a statement with too little information:

Poor Problem Statement 1: *Inventory levels are too high and must be reduced.*

Having high inventory levels is a problem, but a problem statement containing so little information significantly reduces your ability to take a specific action, enlist support, and see improvement.

The problem statement must not include any indication or speculation about the cause of the problem or what actions will be taken to solve the problem. Never attempt to solve the problem or steer the solution at this stage.

Removing bias from the problem statement is one of the ways to prevent individuals from using gut feelings and intuition when trying to solve the problem. Problem statements such as the following are effective at enlisting people's attention, energy, and support:

Better Problem Statement 1: *Inventory levels at the West Metro inventory storage process in Scottsdale are consuming space, taking up asset management time, and creating cash flow issues. Inventory levels are averaging 31 days, with a high of 45 days. These levels have exceeded* *the target of 25 days 95% of the time since January 2022. $250,000 could be saved per year if inventories were at the targeted level.*

Look at the amount of information available in this example. You know where the problem is occurring; you know how long it has occurred; you know the magnitude of the problem, and you know how much it is costing the organization.

Step 2: Identify the "Givens"

Now that you have drafted a problem statement, what's next?

It is time to ask yourself, "What do I already know that could help me ensure this is a real problem of magnitude that others are seeking to solve?" We have coined the term "universal truths" to represent the fundamental facts that support our assumptions and decision. These truths are repeated across multiple sources and are unlikely to change over time. We encourage teams to document what their universal truths are, along with credible sources of information to support the initial framing of the problem. We will talk more about this in our next section, specifically in Chapter 4, called "Patterns."

Once we have documented our facts and what we know to be true, it's time to start making some assumptions. We need to remind ourselves that assumptions are not the same as facts. A fact is something that has occurred or is the case. The usual test for a statement of fact is verifiability—that is, whether it can be proven. An assumption, on the other hand, is an idea or statement that something is true, without proof to back it up.

In his best-selling book *Blink: The Power of Thinking Without Thinking*, Malcolm Gladwell describes how we all make assumptions. Sometimes we get them right, he says. And sometimes we get them wrong. Gladwell says the consequences of making mistaken assumptions can be disastrous, especially in a changing world. In a time of change, there are three things Gladwell says are increasing for all of us in making assumptions:

- The pressure to make decisions in situations we have not encountered before
- The likelihood that any assumptions we make will be based on the way the world *used to* work, not the way it works now
- The size of the negative consequences if we get our assumptions wrong

As we go through the process of making assumptions, there will be questions we will not have answers to yet. A simple way to convert your questions into assumptions is to adopt the technique of framing that says, "We believe that . . ." For example, if the question is:

Why is our cart abandonment rate for shoppers on our online platform higher than the industry norm?

Converting this question into an assumption could read:

We believe our abandonment rate is higher because we do not offer free shipping.

Some assumptions we make may be true; however, without evidence, how do we know? To avoid spreading resources too thin, the focus of your efforts should be only on those assumptions you believe will be critical to the success of solving the problem. We have found a couple of thinking frameworks useful to help teams more deeply understand the nature of the problem and its associated assumptions. These frameworks and applications will be covered in the next section, specifically in Chapter 5, called "Pain Points."

Step 3: Generate Questions

A natural extension of assumptions is to identify what you wish you knew—or what we call IWIKs (I wish I knews). As mentioned, these are simply your unanswered questions. When working with teams, we find this list can get quite long. As part of defining your business problem, use the following guidance to identify and prioritize your IWIKs.

- What would you need to know to validate your assumptions?
- In your problem statement, how confident are you in the data defining the issue?
- What questions are you getting from management?

Next, explore some *why* questions. Why is this happening?

- What causes have been discussed?
- What would you need to know to determine which cause is the primary driver?
- What could you learn to uncover new causes?

The first step in coming up with IWIKs is to gather your evidence—what do you already know about the problem? Start with the data you use to define the problem in part one. Next, add any data you have that connects to your assumptions. Review this data with a cross-functional team to generate a diverse set of questions. When you review data, set clear expectations that the goal is to arrive at questions and that pontification is encouraged. When these sessions are in-person or virtual, we like to have an activity included to guide this discussion. Consider:

- **Have a document available for the team to write questions.** If the session is in-person, print your data on large sheets of paper and have the team add Post-it notes to list their questions. Use the Post-it notes to guide your discussion
- **Create a live document.** We particularly like creating an Excel spreadsheet that is available in SharePoint or some other "live"

link option. List key data/facts/assumptions in columns and assign your teammates a row to respond to. This allows participants to think ahead of the meeting and add comments after the meeting. The benefit of assigning a row is to encourage participation—people don't like to lose and having a blank row will play into that principle

- **Share all the data** as a pre-read and then have a warm-up activity for everyone to write down as many questions as they can think of in three minutes. Use these to guide a debrief

At the end of your IWIK-gathering session, you need to organize and prioritize. We recommend grouping your IWIKs into three categories. The first category is "easy"—what IWIKs could be answered with existing data and minimal effort? Next, split the remaining IWIKs into "critical" and "nice to know." Some will be obvious, whereas others might be debatable regarding their level of impact on the business problem. For those with debate, explore how answering that IWIK will help address the business problem. We like to ask the following questions to facilitate this discussion:

If you had to guess, what is the answer to this question?

If we found out that guess is correct, what would you do?

When our actions aren't clear with the learning, we would argue they are "nice to know."

As you answer the IWIKs from the "easy" category, it is helpful to re-engage the team. Share the information and revisit the IWIKs that remain. Determine if any new IWIKs exist. Next, re-prioritize the remaining IWIKs with these new ones.

There is a fine tradeoff between seeking perfection in the process and gathering evidence and moving on to the next step, which is developing a hypothesis. We recommend having only one follow-up session after you have addressed the "easy" IWIKs, then try the next step. If needed, you can always come back and answer some of the prioritized IWIKs and then try moving to step 4 again. In fact, we recommend thinking of steps 3 and 4 as a cyclical process.

Step 4: Develop Hypotheses

Developing hypotheses is a critical component of the insights process. As described, insights explain why—but the why is not always obvious. In the last section of this book, we will describe a process we call "synthesis." This is simply making connections between data points to generate new thinking. The following framework is one we have found to be most effective in developing hypotheses.

- Because: What evidence is supporting your hypothesis?
- Belief: Start your statement with, "We believe . . ." to describe a hypothesis. What do you believe is the "deep truth" or insight?
- Behavior: What you will do if your hypothesis is proven to be true?

Here is a simple example just to illustrate these three categories for a hypothesis.

- Because: My daughter has mentioned several times that kids in her class don't think Santa Claus is real. She has asked if kids who don't believe in Santa Claus get half as many presents
- Belief: My daughter no longer believes in Santa Claus but doesn't want to receive fewer gifts
- Behavior: If this is true, we would start going on Christmas vacations rather than buying "From Santa" gifts

Generating hypotheses can be difficult for some. When working with a team, we recommend having a few drafted, then obtaining feedback on those hypotheses. Often, these starter hypotheses will also generate new ones from team members. There is no right or wrong answer to determining the number of hypotheses you should have. We recommend having more rather than less since the next step is to prioritize.

Step 5: Prioritize

In this final part of the process, you should have a list of IWIKs and hypotheses. You will also likely have a finite number of resources and a timeline to address these. It is time to pause, reflect, and prioritize. Go back to part one, the problem statement. Here are some questions to guide your prioritization:

- For steps two through four, what have you uncovered about this problem?
- Which IWIKs remain that would help you better understand the problem?
- Which hypotheses do the team feel are most likely and lead to realistic and effective behavior?
- Which IWIKs should you address to validate these hypotheses?

Once you have this step completed, you are ready to develop a plan to gather evidence to answer your IWIKs and validate your hypotheses. It is important to remember this process and any insights investigation is a cyclical process. You need to re-visit your learnings and continue to synthesize, make assumptions, and hypothesize as you address these IWIKs and gather data. This will be covered in Section 3.

To see the full parts of a problem definition, here is an example we like to use when we apply the New Coke case (see Chapter 2).

Part 1: Problem statement

Coke has had a steady share decline, resulting in a 3-point loss over the past ten years and a full-point loss in the last twenty-four months. This is despite a 25 percent increase in advertising spend.

Part 2: Assumptions

The blind taste test is an objective measure of people's preferences. The Pepsi Challenge campaign is having an impact on market share. Creating a drink that tests better than Pepsi in blind taste tests will translate into a higher market share.

Part 3: IWIKs

Why is the blind taste test driving market share?

Are there other tests that evaluate preference?

What has previously driven market share away from Pepsi?

Part 4: Hypothesis

Because: Coke has high equity with consumers.

Belief: We believe the results might be different if the test was unblinded.

Behavior: If this is true, we would focus on equity-building tactics over changing the formula.

Part 5: Prioritization

Most important question is if other types of taste tests have the same results between Coke and Pepsi.

Most of the time, these five parts are enough to address a problem. However, there is a part six—reframing the problem for those situations when it is needed.

Step 6: Reframe the Problem (if needed)

As mentioned in Chapter 2, people can develop a mental fixation and get trapped by the initial framing of the problem. Wedellsborg, in his book *What's Your Problem?*, recommends overcoming this trap by reframing the problem. He says that reframing is about seeing the big picture and having the ability to consider situations from multiple perspectives. It is where you challenge your initial understanding of the problem to uncover potential alternative framings of the problem. Wedellsborg suggests five strategies that can help find these alternative framings of the problem. And depending on the situation, you can explore some, all, or none of these.

- **Look outside the frame.** What are we missing?
- **Rethink the goal.** Is there a better objective to pursue?
- **Examine bright spots.** Where is the problem *not?*
- **Look in the mirror.** What is our role in creating this problem?
- **Take their perspective.** What is their problem?

Once you have considered some alternative framings of the problem, you can choose to continue your current course or move to explore some of the new framings you came up with, or both. You may also choose to validate the framing or reframing of your problem through real-world testing to make sure your diagnosis is correct.

Let's look at a specific case example where understanding the problem to be solved required a reframing of the problem.

CASE: PROCTER & GAMBLE—*"How Febreze Was Brought Back to Life"*

Procter & Gamble (P&G) launched a brand in the US back in 1996 that we all know and use today called Febreze, a spray that removes bad smells from almost any fabric. The spray had been created when one of the P&G scientists was working with a substance called hydroxy propyl beta cyclodextrin (HPBCD). Apparently, he was a smoker, and one day, when he got back home from work, his wife asked, "Did you quit smoking?"

"No," he said.

"You don't smell like smoke," she said.

Enamored with a Solution for an Unrecognized Problem

Based on the scientist's discovery, P&G sensed a big opportunity and spent millions perfecting the formula and producing a colorless, odorless liquid that could make any stinky couch or jacket scentless. The science behind the spray was so advanced that NASA would eventually use it to clean the interiors of shuttles after they returned from space. The marketing team decided they should position Febreze as something that would allow people to rid themselves of embarrassing odors. This is an example of Getzels's problem type #3 as mentioned earlier in this chapter—falling in love with an idea with little evidence the solution solves a real-world problem that customers value or can readily recognize.

The story goes, as told by author Charles Duhigg, the marketing team was so enamored with their new solution and confident the launch of Febreze would be a success, they started projecting what they would buy with their bonuses. It was even mentioned the head of marketing talked about buying a Ferrari not only for himself but also for his girlfriend. However, the launch of Febreze turned out to be one of the greatest launch disappointments in P&G history. Sales were drastically lower than market estimations at launch, and at one point, the company even considered terminating the product. After months had passed and sales continually declined, P&G had concluded they had an official flop but couldn't understand why.

Developing a New Hypothesis

P&G hired behavioral experts to help them figure out the real problem and investigate the *why* by talking to consumers. Duhigg, in *The Power of Habit,* explains that P&G researchers visited a woman in Phoenix who kept a very well-organized house and had nine cats. When the researchers entered the house, the smell of the cats was so overpowering that "one of them gagged," but the woman could not notice the odor. They figured that even the strongest scent fades with constant exposure. P&G's strategy had been to attempt to create a new habit loop incorporating the removal of unpleasant smells as part of the cleaning ritual. Their false assumption was the bad smell would be the cue to start the routine to use Febreze. However, the people who needed Febreze the most simply could not detect unpleasant smells in the first place.

To its credit, P&G did not give up. It hired a Harvard Business School researcher to watch hours of videos of customer interviews and observations of cleaning routines. One woman in Scottsdale, Arizona, provided a clue to the Febreze team. After she cleaned a room in her house, she sprayed the carpet with Febreze—and then enthused, "It's nice, you know? Spraying feels like a little mini celebration when I'm done with a room." At the rate she was going, P&G's team estimated she would empty a bottle of Febreze every two weeks. They saw the same pattern across thousands of hours of videotapes that P&G had accumulated over the years of people cleaning their homes.

Reframing the Problem Using the Habit Loop

After further analysis, P&G realized that it could only succeed with Febreze if it was positioned as part of an existing cleaning routine rather than trying to create a new one. The real Habit Loop was discovered because of this: the observation that people seemed to display moments of happiness upon completion of household chores. It included the cue—a freshly cleaned room; the routine—spraying that room with Febreze, and the reward—relishing "a smell that says you have done a great job."

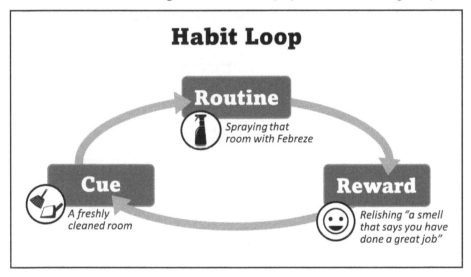

This was the insight that led P&G to alter the product formulation. The team decided to make Febreze a fun part of cleaning, to be used *at the end* of the cleaning routine. They added more perfume, so instead of merely neutralizing odors, Febreze had a distinct smell. Febreze was repositioned as the nice smell that occurs at the end of the cleaning routine. Instead of eliminating scents, it became an air freshener, used as the finishing touch. Febreze was relaunched in 1998. Now, Febreze sales are more than $1 billion (about $3 per person in the US) per year and products include candles, laundry detergents, kitchen sprays, and more. P&G learned a lesson: no one craves scentlessness.

This is a great example of using simple observation to recognize that the initial problem defined was not the true problem to solve. By not giving up and using the additional research exploration, along with the habit loop to reframe the problem, the result was Febreze being saved from termination.

Practice: Follow the Problem Definition Steps

Think about a decision you need to make in the near future. This could be a personal decision (like going back to school or changing jobs), a business decision (like determining if you should move to a new building), or one you need to make as a family (like deciding to buy a new house). Follow the steps we outlined in this chapter.

Step 1: Write down your problem statement.

Step 2: List the facts and assumptions you have made relative to this problem.

Step 3: Generate your questions.

Step 4: Write down at least one hypothesis.

Step 5: Prioritize the information you need to gather to prove your hypothesis/make your decision.

Step 6: Reframe the problem if needed.

SECTION 2:

THE 4 PILLARS—TOOLS TO FINDING INSIGHTS

There was a three-year chunk as a teen
where I should have been tranquilized
and put in a cage.
—Melissa McCarthy, American comedian and actress

"Insights: Taught or Natural-Born Talent"—Melinda

Mitch likes to ask me where I learned how to uncover insights. "Did they teach this in undergraduate or graduate school? Was it developed over time with experience?" The answer is probably yes and yes, as well as no and no. Many of the fundamental principles, data sources, and research approaches we cover in this book are taken from academia and our favorite business books, but the application comes from experience and partnerships—so yes and yes.

Now for the no and no. It is not enough to know the tools and collect the data. You need to practice, and some people will have to practice more than others. I refer to my Aunt Sandi as one of the most insightful people I know. She is not a marketer, a researcher, a therapist, or any profession you would associate with insights. Yet she has the skills needed to apply the tools we will be introducing in this next section. She is analytical, as well as a skilled listener and observer. She is empathetic and calm. She is a mother to three but a caretaker to everyone to whom she is related.

Many of her pithy words of wisdom come back to me as my children get older. I don't mean advice on how to make homemade baby food or discipline when they break curfew.

The words that keep coming back to me, now that I have a teenager and a pre-teenager (i.e., a tween), are "Don't feel guilty about how much you work or going on adult-only vacations when your kids are young—do it now. **You think your kids need you more than they do when they are young, but they actually need you more when you both think they don't.** When your kids get older, you need to be around more." I know this to be true when my kids throw me curve balls and I am forced to reflect on my teenage years. You probably have your own Aunt Sandi—that person you rely on to see the big picture and tell you the truth.

Where Do Insights Come From?

Insights can come from a single statement given on a comment card (in the case of the Trapper Keeper, which we will cover in Chapter 4) or through years of research by insights professionals (in the case of Luv's diapers, covered in Chapter 5). The information required to uncover an insight can be free and readily available or based on extensive and customized market research. For these reasons, insights cannot just be taught, they must be practiced.

Finding insights is not formulaic or linear. There is no standard process. As mentioned earlier, insight generation doesn't follow a timeline. Given these challenges, we saw a need to share tools to aid in the insight discovery process. These tools can be used in isolation but often work best in combination and repeated over time with new information and questions. We will describe these tools as the "4 Pillars."

We chose the term *pillar* to signify that alone, the tool can uncover an insight, but in combination, they strengthen the foundation of your insight. In Chapter 8, we will discuss the process of synthesis, which combines the learnings from more than one pillar to enhance and refine your insight. Before jumping ahead to synthesis, let's introduce the 4 Pillars.

The 4 Pillars are Patterns, Pain Points, Perspectives, and Perplexities.

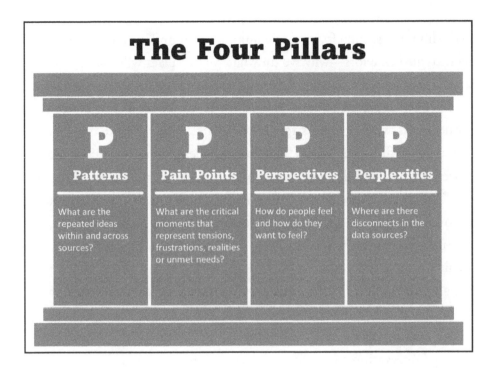

Patterns refers to the ability to uncover consistent conclusions across multiple data sources. Of the 4 Pillars, this one will likely seem the easiest. Most of our analytical tools and the progress of machine learning and artificial intelligence lead to the identification of patterns. The abundance of easily obtainable data can challenge our ability to evolve a pattern into an insight. This section will discuss how to identify patterns as well as how to avoid getting stuck in a common phenomenon we call "analysis paralysis."

Pain Points refers to a term often considered synonymous with insights: *unmet needs*. Unmet needs are difficult because people cannot always tell you what they need. Rather, determining pain points is dependent on the skill of the observer to see what is missing and ask, "What if?" In this section, tools and frameworks for being better observers of behavior will be provided.

Perspectives refers to more than just the emotional element of insights. In this section, we will describe the mindset required to see someone else's perspective. If you are reading this book to uncover insights at a personal level, this is the section for you. Insights are about understanding the "whys" behind our behaviors—why we do what we do. Data will only get you so far. Being able to see the world from someone else's eyes is often required.

Perplexities refers to perhaps our favorite of the tools—embracing disconnects. As we feel more strongly convicted about a topic, we look for data that confirms our beliefs. Data that challenges our conclusions is dismissed or viewed as flawed. This is commonly referred to as "confirmation bias." In all our years of marketing and market research, we have found disconnects to be the sparks needed for finding good insights.

In each chapter in Section 2, we will include our comedy quote, personal story, and a description of the tool, with a case study at the end. We will also highlight a specific critical skill required for this tool. These are:

- Summarizing
- Observation techniques
- Active listening
- The art of asking a great question

CHAPTER 4:
PATTERNS

A conclusion is the place where you got tired of thinking.
—Steven Wright, American comedian

"Misfit or Maverick"—Melinda

Corporations are funny places to me. Perhaps this is because I didn't come from or belong to a large organization or institution. I didn't grow up in a specific religion. I moved constantly during childhood, attending eight different schools across three different states, which means I didn't have a hometown. I even selected a small liberal arts college that most people mispronounce over a big-name school. I lacked roots and affiliation.

Turning twenty-one marked more than the usual milestone. It was the first time I became a part of a large organization by attending the University of Georgia for my master's degree. Following that was my first "real" job as a market researcher, working for a large pharmaceutical company. Constantly meeting new people felt familiar to me while processes, structure, and rules did not. As one boss said to me, "Is it that you are not afraid to break the rules, or are you unaware they exist?" I wish it was the former, but it really is the latter. Fortunately, I had great mentors and leaders that rebranded my lack of fit, calling me a "maverick" rather than a "misfit." Their belief in me led me to hone my approach to patterns, which we will describe in this chapter.

Three years after I joined the pharmaceutical company, we experienced a surprise overturn of a patent. This required a pivot—also called a *reallocation*—also known as layoffs. My position was saved, but my boss and budget were not. For about six months, I didn't have a clear assignment or responsibility. What I did have was a library of data from prior studies, and I was restless. Not having a boss or a defined team with clear objectives meant I was free to do just about whatever I wanted. You would think that would mean I would come in late and leave early. I did the opposite; it was the most I ever worked.

All of my work friends and colleagues were on teams with reduced budgets, which meant they needed help. I had access to data they didn't even know existed. I pulled together reports and presentations to address business questions through a re-analysis of my rag-tag research repository. This gave me access to multiple teams with different business problems and questions.

After a few months, I saw a pattern among these different requests. These patterns allowed me to structure a project with another colleague of mine, Elizabeth, that solved a problem not even senior management recognized existed. This project was one of the most exciting and impactful of my career. It taught me how to influence and sell an idea across an organization. Elizabeth and I grew a graduate school acquaintanceship into what would become one of my most treasured friendships. The end of the project resulted in three things for me: 1) a highly recognized execution that changed the organization and got me a few glass awards for my desk; 2) a developed process for reanalyzing existing data, and 3) the realization I needed to leave the company.

I will always remember that time in my career as an inflection point. I figured out that I loved solving the business challenge but not executing on it—at least not within a large company and as an employee. I also developed the early idea of "data recycling." This is the idea to continue to re-analyze existing data before (or instead of) generating new data. This concept was the foundation for forming my company, Practical Insights. I've taken on too many data recycling projects to even count, and they are still my favorite, setting up for me the most rewarding work I do.

Data Recycling

Re-analyzing data you already have is essential to proper problem definition and insight discovery. Unfortunately, it is undervalued and often penalized in large corporations. Many of our clients are evaluated and incentivized by the execution and completion of new projects. The value of a team in market research is often equated to the size of its budget. Reanalysis of data is resource heavy, but not in a traditional way. Reanalysis requires uninterrupted time that is not conducive to our "meeting-heavy" corporate cultures. For many companies, it is easier to start a new project than to re-evaluate what they already have.

Re-analysis is a discipline. Teams we have worked with that embrace this step almost always become more proficient in insight discovery and end up repurposing a portion of their budget for new, innovative techniques. In this chapter, you will be given tools and techniques to find existing data, organize and document your sources, and, of course, find patterns in the data. Applying what you learn in this chapter should not only enable your insight discovery process—mainly synthesis, which we will discuss in the last section—but also make you more efficient in any activity that requires multiple sources of data.

Data Is Everywhere

Gone are the days of looking up articles on microfiche in libraries—some of you are probably asking, "What is a microfiche?" Now we can just type everything into Google for a quick answer. In most scenarios, this is a blessing. In insight discovery, it can be a curse. It can be easy to search your question, but two challenges can arise. One, being overwhelmed with the number of potential links you search to find your answer, and two, your bias can easily creep in by clicking on the link that most aligns with what you believe is the answer. There are some secondary research tips that can help you with this task.

1. **Create a list of "go-to" sites for your industry.**

Melinda has put together a presentation called "Search Beyond Google" that outlines her go-to sites in health care. This has been a popular topic among our start-up clients on limited budgets. In this talk, she outlines four key sources as her go-tos on any topic. These are social science, testimonials, industry "org" or governments, and competitors' sites. See the table for specific sites related to these categories.

Site Category	Type of information	Example
Social Sciences	Published attitude data	• Pew Research: pewresearch.org • Gallup Poll: gallup.com • Harris Poll: theharrispoll.com
Testimonials/Advocacy	First-hand experience	• youtube.com • patientslikeme.com
Industry "Org"/Government	Generally accepted facts	• cdc.org • who.int
Competitors	Competitive view on the market	• Any competitor's websites • clinicaltrials.gov • centerwatch.com

Each of these go-to categories has a defined purpose to help with a research question. Depending on the question, you may prioritize some sites. Here are some tips for each of the four categories.

Social Sciences: These sources will usually provide attitudes and opinions based on a US representative and projectable sample size. Many of these questions have been asked over several years, providing trend data. The three sites listed in the table are often "go-to" because they will provide more data than just what is published. It is important to look at other questions asked than just those that get picked up in a story, as the author or publication may have a bias.

Testimonials/Advocacy: Never underestimate the power of a good story. Listening to testimonials brings a voice to the question. If you are trying to understand someone's needs or pain points, this is a great place to start. Keep in mind: these are not representative. People tend to share extreme experiences rather than the average. Balancing testimonials with quantitative, representative data, like what was described in social sciences, is important.

Industry "Org"/Government: Having a list of non-profit, industry-related sites can offer a resource of generally accepted facts. In health care, the Center for Disease Control (CDC) has several studies fielded yearly to provide health statistics about a variety of conditions. For any new health-care client we work with, this is our first stop. The CDC site can be almost as overwhelming as a Google search for healthcare topics; however, like the social sciences websites, they often make their datasets available for further analysis. To give a non-healthcare example, CollegeBoard.org is an example of a go-to site for those high schoolers and their parents investigating college options.

Competitors: Sometimes our most painful projects teach us the most. For about three months, Melinda filled in for a competitive intelligence analyst on a launch brand. Every month, she painstakingly looked at competitor websites—for changes in launch dates, language, and tone; clinicaltrials.gov for new advances or any progress made with existing competitor trials; and analysts' reports to see what competitors were saying to analysts about their products. While this was a tedious project, it taught us competitors drop hints about their strategies by what they say (or even what they don't say). Competitors also give away key industry data, which may not be available to all.

2. **Find the original source.**

When you have exhausted your go-to sources, you will often need to go back to the tried-and-true Google search. As you peruse articles, you will inevitably find the holy grail of a fact that is provocative and proves your point. It would be easy to stop there, but that is when we get into trouble.

For any published article that has your key fact, look and see if that fact is referenced. If so, track down the original source. Often the original source is not as definitive as your article claims—and that is okay. It is important to keep your references in context. It just may not be as exciting as you want it to be.

Here is an example from our presentations. We like to share the following statistic: "45% of our daily behavior is habitual." We found this from a very reputable source, the Marketing Society. The author of the original source, Wendy Wood, is an authority on habits. However, going back to the original source of her work gives context to this statistic. It comes from two research studies tied to a diary method of writing down behaviors and then researchers classifying each behavior as habitual or not—a simplistic description of this research methodology. Knowing this context, if anyone challenged this stat, we could describe the study and add the commentary that this is likely underrepresented since many habits are unconscious and may not have made it into the diary.

This is a positive example of the original source adding more clarity to the statistic. More nefarious examples are the subject of many drama series where the key fact is from a biased study or buried memo. Nonetheless, it underscores the importance of getting to the original source.

3. Set a limit.

When you are looking for information, it is easy to get caught in the endless search pages of links. This can cause you to get overwhelmed, frustrated, even exhausted. To avoid this, create a stop point. This could be a time limit or a number of total sources. Once you reach your defined limit, force yourself to stop. Then take a deeper read of everything you have gathered and summarize it (see the end of this chapter for our critical skill: *how to summarize*). As you summarize, note what you feel confident about and what questions you have remaining.

Here is an example from a synthesis we did for a client to understand the prescription market for treating obesity. This is the summary we wrote from an eight-page report from the CDC.

06/15 – https://www.cdc.gov/nchs/data/databriefs/db219.pdf

Prevalence of Obesity Among Adults and Youth: United States, 2011–2014

By: Cynthia L. Ogden, Ph.D.; Margaret D. Carroll, M.S.P.H.; Cheryl D. Fryar, M.S.P.H.; and Katherine M. Flegal, Ph.D.

This report provides the most recent national data on obesity prevalence by sex, age, and race and Hispanic origin, using data for 2011–2014. Overall prevalence estimates from 1999–2000 through 2013–2014 are also presented. Obesity is defined using cut points of body mass index (BMI). BMI does not measure body fat directly, and the relationship between BMI and body fat varies by sex, age, and race and Hispanic origin. Morbidity and mortality risk may vary between different racial and Hispanic origin groups at the same BMI. Some studies suggest that among some Asian subgroups, health and mortality risks may begin at a lower BMI compared with other racial and Hispanic origin groups.

- The prevalence of obesity among U.S. adults remains higher than the Healthy People 2020 goal of 30.5%
- The prevalence of obesity was higher in women (38.3%) than in men (34.3%). Among all youth, no difference was seen by sex
- The prevalence of obesity was higher among middle-aged (40.2%) and older (37.0%) adults than younger (32.3%) adults
- The prevalence of obesity was higher among non-Hispanic white, non-Hispanic black, and Hispanic adults and youth than among non-Hispanic Asian adults and youth
- From 1999 through 2014, obesity prevalence increased among adults and youth

---

As you review your summaries, you can determine if you need to update your source with more recent information or if it is "good enough" and want to address new questions. Continue to set limits to help ensure you are addressing your core purpose and learning new things rather than continuing to validate existing findings.

4. Create a data directory.

If you have ever written a long thesis or term paper, you have learned this lesson already. Creating your reference list from the beginning helps keep you organized and efficient. The approach you take should be customized to your industry, purpose, and the type of data you have. Our go-to approach is to create a table and number each source so you can add as you go. Often, we will add some details in the table that might be helpful. See the image for our obesity example.

ID	Original File Name	Date
01/17	http://www.medscape.com/viewarticle/876411	Mar 2017
02/17	http://medcitynews.com/2017/05/weighing-down-obesity-drug-market/	May 2017
03/16	https://www.statnews.com/2016/05/17/obesity-pill-market/	May 2016
04/17	https://www.fool.com/investing/2017/05/19/the-3-best-obesity-drug-stocks-to-buy-in-2017.aspx	May 2017
05/12	http://healthyamericans.org/report/98/obseityratesbystate	Aug 2012
06/15	https://www.cdc.gov/nchs/data/databriefs/db219.pdf	Nov 2015
07/15	https://www.cdc.gov/obesity/data/prevalence-maps.html	Apr 2015
08/17	http://www.medscape.com/features/slideshow/anti-obesity-drugs#page=3	Jan 2017
09/16	https://www.ncbi.nlm.nih.gov/pmc/articles/PMC5089644/	Jun 2016
10/07	https://www.fda.gov/downloads/Drugs/Guidances/ucm071612.pdf	Feb 2007
11/15	http://www.reuters.com/article/us-novonordisk-saxenda-idUSKBN0ND1KX20150422	Apr 2015
12/12	http://abcnews.go.com/blogs/health/2012/05/07/fat-forecast-42-of-americans-obese-by-2030/	May 2012
13/17	https://contrave.com/content/pdf/Contrave_PI.pdf	May 2017
14/17	http://www.novo-pi.com/saxenda.pdf	May 2017
15/16	https://www.gene.com/download/pdf/xenical_prescribing.pdf	Aug 2016
16/14	https://qsymia.com/patient/include/media/pdf/prescribing-information.pdf	Jan 2014
17/17	https://www.belviq.com/-/media/Files/BelviqConsolidation/PDF/Belviq_Prescribing_information-pdf.PDF?la=en	May 2017
18/15	https://www.guideline.gov/syntheses/synthesis/50302	Feb 2015
19/17	https://clinicaltrials.gov/ct2/results?term=obesity&cond=%22Obesity%22	Jun 2017

As you see in this table, we have given each source an ID number. This ID number is the combination of the number we gave the source in our search, followed by the year the source was published. In this project, we had findings that spanned from 2004 to 2017. Adding the year helped us evaluate our findings in the next step, the synthesis, to know if what we had was dated thinking or repeated over time.

The notes from source 06/15 were shown in tip #3. Here is an example of a graph taken from this project that ties back to this source:

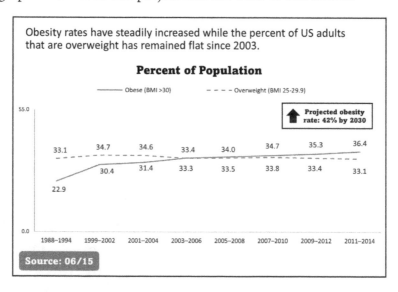

Sometimes you might be given your references. This is often the case we find ourselves in when working with new clients. They have already conducted market research studies, but no one has synthesized the work to document what they already know. Our first step is to take all the "stuff" they already have and consolidate what is known. Depending on the volume of work, we might first create a natural grouping of the references. For example, you might group studies with similar objectives or organize the material based on respondent groups. This will allow you to divide up the references if you are working as a team.

In one of Melinda's larger synthesis projects (she didn't even know Mitch yet), she was part of a team that reviewed well over 200 market research reports from nine countries. Given this volume, the research studies were grouped into five categories: concept testing, attitudes and practices, package testing, positioning, and promotional effectiveness. This grouping allowed for a more manageable table of research type and market location. This helped her and her team determine how to divide up the studies to summarize and have a better picture of what was available.

Finding the Pattern

The first pillar for insight discovery is patterns because to build our knowledge, we must first start with what we already know. You must look for common conclusions across the summaries you've composed. *Patterns refer to the repeated ideas within and across your sources.* These don't have to be 100 percent consistent, but rather similar enough to offer confidence that something is true. When we teach insight discovery, we often refer to these as "universal truths." *Universal truths are the fundamental facts that support our assumptions and decisions.* This process gives you an audit trail of your source and confidence in these facts.

This part of insight discovery might seem elementary, even boring, but it is critical. Insights require assumptions and associations to be made. Confidence in making these connections increases when facts are the foundation.

Patterns are not limited to quantitative data. Here are some quotes from a published qualitative study about the underdiagnosis of COPD (chronic bronchitis and/or emphysema). Read each quote. What is the consistent pattern?

- "Well, no one actually told me I had it. One day, they gave me the Atrovent, and I said 'This is a new one,' and they said, 'That is for your emphysema." (Female patient, 50)
- "I read up in a couple of medical books. I have been like this for two or three years, and no one actually told me I had emphysema." (Female patient, 50)
- "I don't really know that much about it. I haven't really had it explained to me." (Male patient, 55)
- "You don't actually say they have emphysema; they are not keen to have that. They don't like emphysema; they have seen Grandad starved of oxygen. I find they will fight that label." (Female physician)
- "I don't suppose it really matters whether one puts a label to it." (Male physician)

What is the pattern? The first three quotes are from patients. All three describe a lack of clear communication from their healthcare providers about their condition. The next two quotes from physicians describe a reluctance to "label" patients. Overall, the pattern seems to be a reluctance to formally communicate a COPD diagnosis to a patient.

Generally, our process for arriving at patterns as part of insight discovery is grounded in a process Melinda learned from her undergraduate days. Two of her professors, Pamela Maykut and Richard Morehouse, taught a process, detailed in their book, *Beginning Qualitative Research: A Philosophic and Practical Guide.* Their process of analyzing data is referred to as the "constant comparative method." Essentially, they recommend codifying data into "units of meaning," which would be a quote like we have above or an observation. Place each unit on an index card. Once you have all your cards, start with one idea you had when obtaining your information. In our COPD example, it might be "reluctance to label." Then sift through all the cards and determine what could fit into this category. Look at the cards you have left. Create new categories and continue with the process with the remaining cards. After you have your categories, re-read the information in the category. Does it all fit? Is there a better category? After you have refined your groupings, look for relationships between them.

Despite the technological advancements made since Melinda learned this process, we still stick with the "card sort" approach to finding patterns. The difference in our approach is that it includes both quantitative and qualitative data. Further, we emphasize the identification of new questions in addition to conclusions. We often find the new questions are more important than the conclusions themselves.

Sticking with our COPD example, let's add some more data to support our pattern that suggests "physicians are reluctant to label patients." In a separate, published study, researchers found among adult patients with known risk factors for COPD who were actively under the care of a physician that about one in five met the criteria for a formal diagnosis of COPD. Among those patients, only one in three was aware of the possible diagnosis. Now we have both quantitative and qualitative support that physicians are not communicating a COPD diagnosis to their patients. More importantly, we have a new question: *Why are they reluctant?*

Summarize and Expand Rather than Exhaust

Key themes in insight discovery are ***debate*** and ***asking new questions*** rather than perfection and expertise. This is also true for your secondary data search and summary of existing data. Finding the pattern isn't the goal. It is part of the process. Another key piece of advice from Maykut and Morehouse is to engage a team. Working with a team ensures checks and balances on your patterns. Team members can challenge assumptions but also ask new questions and offer new suggestions for sources of information.

The challenge in patterns is to avoid getting overwhelmed by the data and the process. As mentioned with the secondary data tips, creating stop points can help you process the information you already have. In our early days of facilitating insights learning programs, we would introduce the Jacob Wetterling story to illustrate this point.

In 1989, eleven-year-old Jacob Wetterling went missing after being abducted while riding home from a video store with his younger brother and best friend. This mystery would haunt the small community of St. Joseph, Minnesota—if not the entire state—for decades. After twenty-seven years and more than 50,000 tips, the person responsible was convicted. A man who had a history of abducting and abusing young boys was within a short drive away from the kids' location. This was not the perfect crime. The mistakes in solving this case are still debated in podcasts, books, websites, and news stories. What fascinated us for an insights class is the danger of too much data. We find a bias that says if we keep searching, that perfect piece of data will become available—we just have to find it.

True crime is riddled with the storyline of the novice investigator taking a "fresh look" at the case. This is not a surprise to us. We get exhausted by data. To make sense of what we have, we look for shortcuts. It is natural. Either missing connections, allowing confirmation bias to creep in, or simply being overwhelmed are the reasons we encourage the notion of stop, summarize, debate for new inquiry, and re-investigate rather than trying to exhaust all the ideas on a single research question. We also recommend engaging a team with a mix of experiences on your topic—which should include a novice or fresh mind.

Critical Skill: Summarization

Chances are when you hear the word *summarize*, you think of high-lighters, Post-it notes, tape flags, and bullet points. These are often our go-to tools for summarizing information—but what gets highlighted or noted is where we can struggle. Often, when we first start with a highlighter, most of the page is yellow. Then, as we move on, less and less gets highlighted as we become exhausted or question what is truly important. We propose a systematic approach when attempting to summarize your sources that should be customized based on the volume of data you have available.

1. **Creating a data directory within your data directory.**

As mentioned earlier in this chapter, we recommend creating a data directory. This is a list of your sources so you can go back and reference your data. Once you have this directory, you will need to summarize each source, as we explained earlier in this chapter. When your number of sources reaches a certain threshold—ours is around fifteen—create another layer to the directory. This helps catalog the information you have before you actually note the specific data points. Let's say you have fifteen sources. Start with the first source and list what is in the source before you summarize the learning.

This step may seem extra but has proven to be a time-saver throughout our projects. We typically create a source template. If you are working with a team, you can divide up the sources and fill out the template. This will be your next step, following the creation of the data directory. Below is an example of a template we have used for a large project involving about thirty sources.

Report #015	
File Name:	Physician Attitude Tracker
File Date:	February 2020
Customer Type:	Primary Care Physicians
Countries:	US, Japan, Germany, Italy, Spain
Report Type:	Multi-wave tracking study
Objective:	Measure changes in attitude and use over time; Measure progress to marketing objectives

Page 2: Sample description
Page 3: Summary/scorecard of progress to marketing objectives
Page 4: Unaided awareness of brands
Page 5: Aided awareness of brands
Page 6: Stated brand use
Page 7: Stated brand use by scenario
Page 8: Anticipated brand use in next 6 months
Page 9: Attitudes toward diagnosis
Page 10: Perceived treatment barriers

As you can see in this example, there are no data or conclusions listed. Rather, it is an expanded table of contents, listing the types of data in the report. Once you have this type of information for all of your sources, you can go back to your original research question/problem statement and start pulling relevant information based on these directories of each report.

When we skip this step as a research team, we always regret it. There are two reasons for this: 1) We end up going back to these sources for future problem statements, and 2) our summaries get progressively worse as we move through the sources, especially when we have more than fifteen of them.

2. **Cull your sources.**

When you have multiple sources to reference for a specific problem or question, cull down the relevant data you want to review. When you are familiar with the data sources already, you may be able to pull the relevant pages from your data directory. In other cases, you may need to skim or read the source to determine if it addresses your need. You may be tempted to pull out that highlighter but resist the urge. Be sure you have all the relevant sources first. When we are doing this step, we often make hard copies and note the reference number on each copy.

3. **Creating a source summary.**

Now you are ready to summarize. As you review each source, keep yourself honest about what data or information addresses your problem statement or research question. This is much harder than it sounds for those inquisitive minds that like fun facts. We will sometimes challenge ourselves to limit the summary to one page. Our most preferred way at this stage is to note key facts and information on cards. This can be done on paper, such as with traditional note cards, or electronically. Often, we will create ours in PowerPoint and then print them out. Below are two examples from our chronic obstructive pulmonary disease (COPD) work. You will see both cards come from the same source, so we added the –1 and –2 after the "Source 6" notation to represent two different data points.

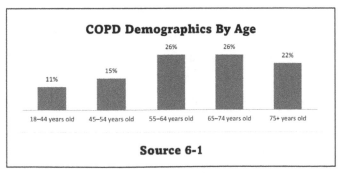

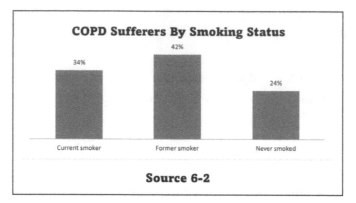

Source 6-2

Electronic cards can be helpful when you have data in charts, graphs, or other visuals since we more often process a picture rather than a bullet point. We will continue to reference the COPD data cards in other chapters that follow.

When you don't have visual data, it can be harder and more time-consuming to summarize. For larger sources, break down the content that summarizes each section. Think about how you would describe the learning in a brief conversation with someone who is not familiar with COPD. This will help keep you focused on the most important points.

In any summarizing activity, it will be hard to avoid making conclusions or assumptions or uncovering new questions. This is all part of the process. We recommend noting these in your summary.

Question—*Would people (the general public and physicians) be surprised that 1/3 of patients suffering from COPD are current smokers? Would they expect it to be higher or lower?*

Hypothesis—*A patient who has successfully quit smoking further hinders a physician from diagnosing COPD because they don't want the patient to be discouraged and start smoking again.*

Our final tip is to keep going back to your problem statement/research question—and keep your summary to only what is relevant. *Physically* write it down and keep it in front of you if necessary.

CASE: TRAPPER KEEPER—"A Success Story Using a Tried-and-True Approach"

We often hear research and the insight discovery process can stifle creativity. While there are examples of invention and design coming from serendipity combined with sheer genius, there are also examples of people following a process. The design of the Trapper Keeper represents all the key pieces we look for in insight discovery:

- A strong situation analysis
- Cross-functional feedback
- Evolving research plan from multiple perspectives
- Tangible and intangible needs

The Trapper Keeper by Mead is as synonymous with 1980s culture as shopping malls and MTV. Here is an outline of the information-gathering steps that informed the development of a back-to-school supply that resulted in approximately $100 million in sales a year and, at the time of the inventor's passing (E. Bryant Crutchfield), 75 million sold.

Source 1: A Situation Analysis

The process to develop the Trapper Keeper started in 1972 with an analysis of trends in the marketplace that showed an increase in students per classroom, an increase in the number of classes those students were taking, and smaller lockers.

A few years later, Crutchfield made a connection to this trend report with a statistic that portfolios and folders were increasing at a rate of 30 percent per year. Of course, kids were buying more folders; they had more classes. How could Mead make a notebook that could accommodate all this data?

Source 2: Cross-Functional Feedback

The next connection for Crutchfield came when he spoke with his West Coast sales representative who suggested the pockets on the folders be vertical rather than horizontal. For whatever reason, folders with vertical pockets were limited to being sold on the West Coast. Crutchfield questioned why this was a benefit. As the sales rep explained, when you have vertical pockets, the paper gets "trapped" inside. Horizontal pockets meant papers would fall out when you held the folder upside down—*anyone that has kids knows they are going to have papers fall out of an upside-down folder.*

Source 3: Corroborating Evidence: Teachers

Crutchfield began the design of a portfolio (folders) and notebooks (binders). As he worked on the mock-ups, he confirmed the need in the market from a most reliable source: teachers. They expressed student organization was a problem, and they welcomed any help a product could offer.

With that, the design evolved from horizontal to vertical pockets. Further, the pockets had information like a ruler and a multiplication table. With a final mockup ready to go, he just needed a name. The concept of "trapping" the papers led to the folders being called Trappers and the notebook, the Trapper Keeper.

Source 4: Ongoing Market Research

For about a year, Crutchfield conducted focus groups and interviews with students and parents, all with the purpose of updating the design to meet their needs. Crutchfield estimates the design evolved over five or six iterations before it was ready for a test market.

Test markets often include an early advertising campaign that runs in specific markets to test the sales potential of the product. In addition to sales, this is a chance to gather real-world experience feedback from those using the product. The Trapper Keeper followed this approach. In August 1978, the Trapper Keeper was rolled out in Wichita, Kansas. Each Trapper Keeper was sold with a few Trapper folders and a feedback card. If a kid returned the feedback card, they would receive a free notebook.

Crutchfield estimates receiving 1,500 comment cards. One of the main questions on the card was, "Why did you purchase the Trapper Keeper rather than another type of binder?" Comments supported the original purpose of the design. "So when kids in my class throw it, the papers won't fly all over." "Instead of taking the whole thing you can take only one part home." Their favorite comment came from a fourteen-year-old: "Keep all my sh*t, like papers and notes." What kids might lack in organization, they make up for in honesty.

Source 5: Tap into More than Function

In 1981, the Trapper Keeper had a national launch that was met with huge success for Mead. Over the years, the functional design has changed very little. The visual design, however, evolved with the times. New styles were rolled out annually. Designs ranged from local artists to licensed images, which took the Trapper Keeper from a functional product to an expression of who the owner is, allowing them to express some individuality.

In Chapter 6, we will describe the importance of uncovering how people want to feel as an important aspect of insight discovery. The Trapper Keeper did just that. Not only did it create a superior product to meet the needs of students, but it also connected with how students want to feel. They want to express themselves, be unique yet still fit in. With their designs, the Trapper Keeper became like a welcome gift instead of a boring school necessity.

Patterns are about seeing the simple connections in data and arriving at truths.

Truth: Kids are disorganized.

Truth: Folders will get thrown.

Truth: Kids want to be their version of "cool."

These truths existed in the late 1970s and 1980s, and they exist today. While the Trapper Keeper has had somewhat of a resurgence in the 2020s because of a growing fascination with 80s culture and because these truths still exist, it is not as popular as it once was. New truths exist for our students.

New Truth: The world has become digitized.

The concern is less about papers flying out of the folder but keeping their devices charged. For this reason, we may continue as insight investigators to ponder the same questions, but we must be prepared for different answers to uncover those new truths that will evolve our thinking and application of insights.

Practice: Disciplined Googling

Next time you find yourself googling, try the stop, summarize, debate for new inquiry, and re-investigate the process.

- Step 1: Set a limit of how long you will allow yourself to search
- Step 2: Once you hit that limit, summarize what you have found
- Step 3: Share what you found with someone else—specifically, someone who will question or debate you
- Step 4: Re-investigate based on a new question from the debate and repeat the process
- Step 5: Evaluate the process. Did it work for you? Was it more satisfying than hours clicking on links? Did you learn anything unexpected?

CHAPTER 5:
PAIN POINTS

How did we get to the point where we're paying for bottled water?
That must have been some weird marketing meeting over in France.
Some French guys sitting there, like, how dumb do we think the
Americans are? I bet you we could sell those idiots water.
—Jim Gaffigan, American comedian

"Someone Is Quitting on Monday"—Melinda

At the beginning of 2007, I fit the description of "having it all." I was just going back to work after having our first child. It was the job I loved and had been striving for. I had been promoted to join the executive team. There were four of us: the two owners of the company, my previous boss (the CFO), and me. These three executives listened to me, respected me, treated me like a peer, and gave me the autonomy I desired. We were all excited about the future of the company, which had aggressive growth plans and a new, beautiful office space.

The first few months after maternity leave were not without challenges. I had to resume traveling while also trying to nurse. Working late meant I might miss bedtime—but not the 2 a.m. feeding. I was exhausted in a way I did not know was possible, but every parent understands.

Despite these new adjustments, it was more than manageable for the first three months because my husband took full paternity leave. In the last few weeks of his leave, we began the transition to daycare. At this point, our son was almost six months old. We knew it would be hard, but this seemed like the right decision. We liked the daycare. The staff was loving and kind. Any parent reading this knows what is about to come—the constant illnesses.

My husband's job required travel as well. So we already knew the scheduling challenges we were about to have. What we didn't anticipate was the constant curve balls of solo parents with a child that was constantly getting sick. One of us would be out of town with the other juggling their work while taking care of a sick child. This, of course, meant working in the evenings and making up work on the weekends when the other person got home.

The unpredictability was the real problem. We would go weeks with a normal routine of drop-offs and pickups with just snotty noses and drooling faces. We would falsely think to ourselves, *We got this.* Sure, our careers have added complexity, but we are smart, overachieving people. We can figure this out. Plus, we are not the first parents to work and have a kid.

Two significant events caused my breaking point. The first was when our son was seven months old. I had wanted to nurse him for a year. Everything I had read said this was the right thing to do. Plus, nursing our son was a way to relieve some of the guilt I had by spending time away from him while I was working. Months four through six were a challenge with going back to work, but my husband was home and able to supplement with formula when needed. When I traveled, I regularly pumped to maintain supply.

Then, on a trip to San Diego, I was sitting on my hotel bed, trying to pump. Nothing would come out. I tried everything. Looking at pictures of my son, watching videos of him, even trying to "talk" to him on the phone. Nothing worked. I bawled. My husband consoled me, saying that once I got home, everything would be back to normal. It wasn't. My body had given up. I could not stop thinking that work had determined this, not me as a parent. I wasn't in control of being the type of parent I wanted to be.

The second event happened not even a month later when my husband was on a business trip and our son was once again sick. I was sitting with him in the doctor's office, getting instructions on how to use a nebulizer, when our pediatrician said something like, "I'm really concerned with how often he has been sick. You may need to consider a different daycare option if he gets sick again." As an emotional, sleep-deprived, overachieving, hormonal, first-time parent, I heard, "The daycare and your career are killing your son."

We got in the car to head to the pharmacy, and a switch flipped in my head. Something had to change. Any delusion I had of "having it all" with a career and family was gone. This was not sustainable for any of us.

My husband returned home that Friday. I gave him one of my "this is serious" looks and said, "We need to have a conversation before the end of the weekend. I don't care when, as long as it happens before Sunday night. One of us is quitting on Monday."

Sunday during naptime my husband said, "Okay. I'll quit. You love your job, and I really loved my time at home. I'll quit on Monday." I knew he would say that, but I had another idea. If he stayed home, I would resent the time he was getting with our son, and I would not love my job anymore. I also knew I had to work. This was when I proposed starting our company, Practical Insights. I believed I could work half as much and make the same amount of money if I consulted. I had always planned to be a business owner one day; I just didn't think it would happen this way. On that Monday, I talked with my management about my plans. I also agreed to consult with them while I got started to make the transition.

Making this choice felt empowering. I would like to say I used all my skills in problem definition and identifying pain points to come up with this solution. It was not that contrived. Instead, it was as if the solution had always been there, and I finally realized it. When we were sitting in our lawyer's office to file the paperwork for the business, my husband said, "This is Melinda's reward for working so hard for everyone else. She will now be in control of her work for herself."

That is when I realized the pain point was not really becoming a mom and seeing the challenges of balancing career and family; it was the pain point of not having control over my workload.

There's Got to Be a Better Way

nsights from pain points are a major source of innovation and new products. If you ever watch the show *Shark Tank*, a common line from entrepreneurs in their pitch is, "There's got to be a better way." This is the essence of a pain point. The next line is often, "Stop the madness," which sets up the product as the solution to the pain point.

What makes pain points difficult is most people can't tell you what they need. Further, people typically create workarounds to ease their pain points. Think about if you ever had to wear a splint or boot after an injury. If so, you learn quickly to compensate in your day-to-day life. At best, customers can recognize frustrations, but they usually cannot tell you what would effectively ease that frustration.

For these reasons, identifying pain points almost always comes from observation. Therefore, our strategic skill and practice at the end of this chapter will be providing tools and techniques for becoming better observers to identify pain points.

Before learning how, we want to provide two thinking frameworks to help structure your pain point discovery. These are *customer journey mapping* and *jobs-to-be-done*. From our experience, one or both of these frameworks have landed within our clients' brand planning activities because they are effective at helping unpack the pain points such that we can connect brands, products, and services as solutions. As with any framework, the application is only as good as the users' proper understanding of the intent and application. Consider the next several sections as your primer on these frameworks. If you would like more information, we encourage you to read the references provided in the Endnotes.

Framework #1: Customer Journey Mapping

Customer journey mapping (CJM) is a diagnostic tool that has been used by many businesses as a strategic exercise to help identify how a customer views an organization, product, or service. It is a process that helps you better understand your customer's experience throughout their buying process. It's not just a generalized idea of your audience, either. Proper customer journey mapping relies heavily on an insightful view of the minds and behaviors of your target audience. At its core, customer journey mapping is a method of developing empathy for your target audience. Proper use of the CJM tool is designed to put the interactions with a company in the context of the customer's broader activities, goals, and objectives. The output often includes an easy-to-understand visual story with a focus on a series of events that comprise a person's experience. The format allows for a deeper understanding of the customer problem(s) and whether we have clearly defined it by mapping the following elements of the experience:

1. WHAT they are doing at each stage of the journey: needs, actions, and decisions
2. WHY they are doing or not doing things: expectations
3. HOW they feel: emotions

The level of detail needed for these maps depends on what you are trying to accomplish.

Patient Journey Example

Since the majority of our work has been in health care and the pharma industry, let's look at how a journey is mapped in this space as an example. CJMs are referred to as *patient journeys* in health care. It is called a patient journey because the one common denominator throughout the entire experience is the patient. It captures an understanding of the patient's experience with a medical condition, from the first symptoms on, and how this condition impacts them in the context of their life. The journey includes the timing, sequence, and details of major events and decisions made along their life journey as they experience their specific medical condition. It's depicted visually as a "map" that illustrates the customer's experiences in a usable way.

These journeys typically focus on a specific patient segment and reflect their perspective (including the physical and emotional aspects of what they feel, struggle with, and hope for) on what they experience as they deal with their health condition(s). The quality of a journey is highly dependent on the quality and articulation of the patient's perspective and the influence of others. Since patients interact with others along their journeys—such as healthcare providers, insurance companies, and caregivers—it should also capture their perspectives, tensions, and frustrations, including those that may occur because of interactions or influence from others.

Moment of Truth

During the patient journey, there are "pain points," or times often referred to as "moments of truth" (MoTs) or "moments of meaning" (MoMs). These are critical moments in the journey, such as emotional revelations or physical events. They may be characterized by tension, frustration, realities, or unmet needs. This is where potential insights live and where hypothesis generation begins. These moments or events may lead to a decision (either consciously or unconsciously) to go in one direction or another. They may stem from the patient, a healthcare provider, or a payer of services. MoTs should be documented. We encourage the MoT to be written in the first-person perspective and begin with the words, "The moment I . . ."

A company or brand may be able to impact some moments, yet likely not all. The opportunity comes with your prioritizing MoTs to focus your efforts based on a realistic assessment of (a) the magnitude of the related customer's tensions/needs and whether you have defined a problem that is worth solving for them, (b) your ability to resolve it (through engagement strategies that are valuable to customers), and (c) the potential to generate the revenue needed for viable business operations.

Once the MoTs are prioritized to help focus your efforts, it's critical to dig deeper into the MoTs to uncover and focus on the specific problem or issue that is not being addressed by others. This enables us to effectively generate ideas for creating customer-centric solutions. When we drill down within a MoT, we dimensionalize (i.e., provide depth) to the situation of the customer in a certain phase of their journey.

If we do not, and we attempt to generate solutions for problems not fully in focus, we may find it difficult to come up with compelling solutions or create solutions that are "one size fits none."

Developing and Communicating a Patient Journey

1. Outline the story.

Often, we have seen companies conduct a patient journey research project. While these market research studies have become areas of expertise for several companies, you can also gather stories from a variety of other sources that range in quality and cost. We like to start with any unstructured testimonials. These can come from YouTube videos, documentaries, memoirs, social media, and patient advocacy groups. Immerse yourself in these patient stories.

After you complete this step, outline what is common in their stories. What was the common path? Give each section a name. Within that section, what is the patient experiencing and feeling? What are they doing? Who are they interacting with? You can then apply primary market research as needed to fill any gaps.

2. Write the story.

Next, as best you can, transition the outline into a full story. Where you can, use the patient's words, not yours. Remember this should be their story. Give each character a name and context. Make them relatable, as if they are a close friend or family member.

Often, this step is skipped because we feel the pressure of time, and it can be a bit uncomfortable. Yet, when this is done as a concentrated effort, the story can be powerful and rich. Melinda wrote one of these for a team where the final product was developed into an ebook that every member of the team, including the sales representatives, had to read. The lead character, the patient, is referred to in meetings by name as if they are a real person in our lives.

3. Map the journey.

Once you have the story, create a visual that maps the critical moments in the journey. These should include the key points along the journey, prioritized moments of truth, and important interactions with others. Below is a simple illustration of a patient with chronic obstructive pulmonary disease (COPD) and their journey from first symptoms to diagnosis.

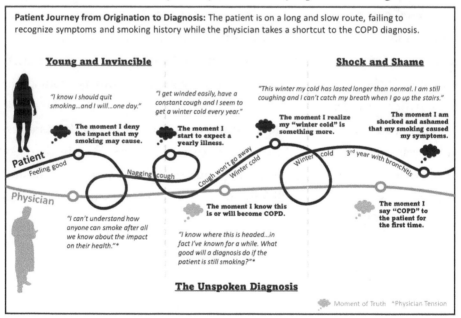

Patient Journey from Origination to Diagnosis: The patient is on a long and slow route, failing to recognize symptoms and smoking history while the physician takes a shortcut to the COPD diagnosis.

A few key aspects of this map are:

- The three key phases from Step 1 are included and given a title: Young and Invincible, The Unspoken Diagnosis, and Shock and Shame. Notice how these three phases are given titles that expresses or imply an emotion. In Chapter 6, we will go into more detail on how to uncover these emotions

- The visual of the lines for the patient and the physician depict the summary statement at the top of the journey map. The patient is on a long and slow route, failing to recognize symptoms and the effects of their smoking history, while the physician takes a short-cut to the COPD diagnosis. People are more likely to remember a picture than a statement. Having a visual within the map to tie to the overall experience helps make the map more memorable and applicable to a broader team
- The moments of truth are supported with quotes. These will serve as the foundation for exploring a pain point

It is at this stage we encourage teams to unpack the priority MoT(s) to articulate needs at even deeper levels using the jobs-to-be-done (JTBD) framework. Essentially, the moment of truth represents a pain point, and the job-to-be-done helps identify how to activate your brand, product, or company as a solution.

Framework #2: Jobs-to-Be-Done (JTBD)

As mentioned, MoTs tend to provide us with only a high-level perspective on the customer's current experience when a more rigorous understanding of the customer perspective is required for effective solution development.

In the early 1980s, one of the founding thinkers of marketing, Theodore Levitt, wrote, "People don't want to buy a quarter-inch drill, they want a quarter-inch hole." He argued that customers are not looking for products; they are looking for solutions. This influential quote has graced many boardroom slide presentations, influencing companies to think deeper about their core purposes. Do they exist to make a product? Or do they exist to enable the customer to achieve some underlying goal? Companies that look at the underlying human needs, goals, and jobs vastly increase their chance of long-term, sustainable profit. This line of thought runs through the history of marketing and business strategy to the highly influential late Harvard Business professor Clayton Christensen. It was Christensen who first coined the term *jobs-to-be-done* in his 2003 book *The Innovator's Solution.*

Christensen defined a job as a fundamental problem that a person faces and for which he or she is (consciously or subconsciously) seeking a solution. Jobs-to-be-done (JTBD) can have functional, social, and emotional elements, or some combination of the three. You may be asking yourself at this point, "What is the difference between a job and a need?" A job is typically at a deeper level and is directly associated with functional, social, and/or emotional characteristics linked to the need. They can be described as the following:

Functional Jobs = jobs seeking solutions that **serve a practical purpose,** e.g., "Help me find a reliable way to get to work." These jobs are often obvious and tangible and where we find teams primarily focus their time and energy. However, it becomes much more difficult to differentiate a brand if a market or category is crowded and the primary functional jobs-to-be-done are already satisfied. Perhaps this is where the JTBD framework is most helpful because it provides two additional dimensions that can be considered for differentiation beyond the functional dimension of a product or service—emotional and social.

Emotional Jobs = jobs seeking solutions that **impact my feelings,** e.g., "Help me ensure my family is safe." As stated in Chapter 1, good insights will normally have an emotional component. Teams struggle with the activation of an emotional insight when it comes to solution generation because emotions are typically deemed "soft" and intangible. The question we often entertain is "How do we activate an emotional insight?" The JTBD framework helps provide a way and a thought process to take something intangible and tie it to the tangible benefit of a brand to arrive at a bigger idea to move beyond the functional level. The emotional job helps teams think about how people want to feel when they use their product or service and what additional aspects of the product experience will be needed to impact their feelings. This will be illustrated with the Luv's case at the end of Chapter 6.

Social Jobs = jobs seeking solutions that **involve other people**, e.g., "Help me convey my status to others." Like emotions, social jobs are not always obvious or tangible on the surface. When people are trying to achieve a particular job, it often requires others to be involved in some way. We will illustrate this one as a part of the Cialis case at the end of this chapter.

When writing a JBTD, we recommend starting with the words *"Help me . . ."* to force ourselves to think from the end-user's point of view.

Christensen explains there's an important difference between determining a product's function and its job. "Looking at the market from the function of a product really originates from your competitors or your own employees deciding what you need," he says. "Whereas the jobs-to-be-done point of view causes you to crawl into the skin of your customer and go with them as they go about their day, always asking the question as they do something: Why did they do it that way?"

Let's look at the late Christensen's famous "milkshake example," which he routinely used with his students at Harvard to illustrate the JTBD concept.

Example: Jobs-to-Be-Done—*"Hiring a Milkshake"*

Christensen used to share in his MBA course the story of a fast-food restaurant chain that wanted to improve its milkshake sales. The company started by segmenting its market both by product (milkshakes) and by demographics (a marketer's profile of a typical milkshake drinker). Next, the marketing department asked people who fit the demographic to list the characteristics of an ideal milkshake (thick, thin, chunky, smooth, fruity, chocolatey, etc.). The would-be customers answered as honestly as they could, and the company responded to the feedback. But alas, milkshake sales did not improve.

The company then enlisted the help of one of Christensen's fellow researchers, who approached the situation by trying to deduce the "job" that customers were "hiring" a milkshake to do. First, he spent a full day in one of the chain's restaurants, carefully documenting who was buying milkshakes, when they bought them, and whether they drank them on the premises. He discovered that 40 percent of the milkshakes were purchased first thing in the morning by commuters who ordered them to go.

The next morning, he returned to the restaurant and interviewed customers who left with a milkshake in hand, asking them what job they had hired the milkshake to do.

"Most of them, it turned out, bought [the milkshake] to do a similar job," he writes. "They faced a long, boring commute and needed something to keep that extra hand busy to make the commute more interesting. They weren't hungry yet but knew that they'd be hungry by 10 a.m.; they wanted to consume something now that would stave off hunger until noon. And they faced constraints: they were in a hurry; they were wearing work clothes, and they had (at most) one free hand."

The milkshake was hired in lieu of a bagel or doughnut because it was relatively tidy and appetite-quenching and because trying to suck a thick liquid through a thin straw gave customers something to do with their boring commute. This would be classified as a "functional" job-to-be-done. Understanding the job-to-be-done, the company could then respond by creating a morning milkshake that was even thicker (to last through a long commute) and more interesting (with chunks of fruit) than its predecessor.

Evaluating when milkshakes are also commonly purchased would be to serve as a special treat for young children—without making the parents wait a half hour as the children tried to work the milkshake through a straw. This job-to-be-done could be considered a "social," and maybe even an "emotional job" too, for parents to do. In that case, a different, thinner milkshake was in order.

There can be many jobs trying to be done by a specific customer segment within a MoT, so the approach should be to prioritize the jobs that are most important, most unsatisfied, and most widely held.

By using the JTBD framework, we can articulate the need in a deeper and more meaningful way to further inform insight and solution generation that might otherwise go unnoticed. Most companies and product managers are good at articulating a functional need, and that's fine when a category is not crowded. However, if you are in a crowded and competitive space where the functional jobs are already satisfied, then you must go deeper to connect with customers on an emotional or social level for differentiation purposes. This is when the JTBD framework can be most helpful in translating emotional and social needs, which teams sometimes struggle in identifying. Often, this is where rich insights are born and can go unnoticed.

Melinda's Moment of Truth and Job-to-Be-Done

Let's go back to Melinda's story at the beginning of the chapter. Imagine you are running a human resource department and read the McKinsey 2022 Women in the Workplace report, which states, "For every woman at the director level who gets promoted to the next level, two women directors are choosing to leave their company." Melinda's story could represent the journey of a working mother who leaves a senior role. The title of her story, "Someone is Quitting on Monday," is an example of a moment of truth. At the end of the story, Melinda realizes what she needed was control over her workload—this is one of her jobs-to-be-done. It is an emotional job that human resource departments have struggled to create realistic solutions for over the years. Perhaps it is because they try to fix the problem by looking at the job from a functional component—drop the hours. Sure, shifting from a full-time position to a part-time position is a solution. What Melinda didn't share in her story is that her management offered her a part-time role. She knew that was not a realistic solution. In a service business where time is billed by the hour, working less within a company—especially in a management role—feels hypocritical. This is not to suggest Melinda's solution is right for everyone. Rather, it is an example of how the moment of truth and job-to-be-done work together to ideate solutions beyond the surface level. In the next chapter, we will cover in greater detail how to go about uncovering how people feel. Melinda's story is a great example of how her perspective facilitated a better understanding of her pain point.

Critical Skill: Observation Techniques

As mentioned earlier in this chapter, the biggest challenge with pain points is the person's ability to recognize and describe them. Sometimes they are obvious, but more often, they are just dealt with. For this reason, our critical skill for this chapter is *observation techniques.*

The best place to start with any observational activity is to understand ethnography, a research tool taken from anthropology. Perhaps the best-known example of ethnography is Jane Goodall's research on chimpanzees. In the context of insight discovery, ethnography is a research design that includes observation and interviewing to understand a group of people and/or activity from their perspective. While some researchers will slap this label to dress up traditional one-on-one interviewing techniques, a true ethnography studies a subject from multiple perspectives over an extended period for a full picture. Primarily, ethnography research is difficult for two significant reasons: 1) to be done well, the "data" needs to be collected in a natural setting, and 2) the researcher is the data collection instrument.

Data in the natural setting means you are unobtrusively collecting data about your subject. In an ideal sense, the researcher is watching without the subject being affected by the observation. In the days of informed consent and privacy, this becomes increasingly difficult. As a result, applying multiple approaches can gather a wealth of data to constitute the true purpose of ethnography—to understand from others' perspectives. The following are sources and approaches to consider with the recommendation to apply more than one:

- Social media listening: what is your subject posting?
- YouTube videos: has anyone shared a personal story?
- Documentaries, autobiographies, and memoirs: has someone else reported on this subject?
- Observation: can you watch the subject or scenario live or on video?
- Participation: can you ethically and unobtrusively become a part of a group or activity?
- Interview: can you talk to your subject, particularly in their environment?

Regardless of your sources, collecting the needed data is dependent on your skill to pick up on the non-obvious obvious. Here are some guiding approaches and tools to help you be a better observer:

1. **Stay true to their language.** What words are being used? Be careful not to paraphrase with your words; rather, keep them to the language of who you are observing. Write your notes in the third person. In our experiences in health care, we often find a mismatch between the clinical description of a condition and the patient's actual description of their experiences with the condition. Reconciling this language discrepancy can often remove unrealized barriers driving misdiagnosis and suboptimal treatment.

2. **Look for inefficiencies.** As mentioned, we often create work-arounds to fix our pain points but don't always realize it. For example, have you ever gone to a store expecting to only buy a few items, so you skip the basket or cart at the store entry, then find yourself at the back of the store struggling to carry your "extra" items? You have two choices: go back to the front of the store and grab a basket or cart or return items and buy less. If you work for the store, you do not want the customer to choose either of these options. Rather, you want there to be an immediate solution so the customer can

keep shopping. Perhaps this is why large retailers, like Target, have baskets located throughout the store. As the researcher/observer, think about what you would observe to identify this pain point. Put yourself in the shoes of the shopper and make note of the inefficiency of returning to the front of the store or the inefficiency of overloading your arms.

3. **Make note of the outliers.** Observe not just the average behavior, but the person who is doing things differently. Why are they different from the others? Did they figure out a solution that others have not? Our example here is the ride-on luggage options for kids. If you have ever traveled with kids, you know this to be pure genius. Kids, at some point, get too big for a stroller but are too little to keep up with their parents. Before the ride-on suitcase became a real product, we had observed parents having their children climb on top of their roller bag and hang on to the handle. The kid has a little fun, and the parent can move faster through a busy airport. This is a workaround but not the average workaround. It is the outlier. When you observe someone who is an outlier, ask, "Why are they different? What is the benefit or drawback of their difference compared to the average?"

4. **Notes should be words and visuals.** Drawing can be uncomfortable for some, but it can help you interpret and analyze what you observe. Again, taking a tip from Maykut and Morehouse in *Beginning Qualitative Research*, they advise you to draw a diagram of the physical layout of the space you are observing. In this layout, detail the following: where do people stand/sit, and where do they not stand/sit? What is the traffic pattern of the space? What objects are people interacting with and which are being ignored? These visuals and corresponding notes will provide context and direction when you explore *why* as possible pain points. Another favorite travel example is the gate area. Think about the experience of people waiting to board a flight and those getting off of the flight that

just arrived. Those wanting to board are standing around (likely impatiently) and edging closer to the boarding area the closer it gets to the boarding time. This is often at the same time arriving passengers are trying to exit the plane. This area can be chaotic. Drawing the space would help identify and describe this chaos. Next time you notice an airline, likely Southwest, having a defined standing area for those passengers to organize the boarding process, think about why this was done and how the experience would be different without this structure.

5. **Don't jump to a solution but explore it.** Many of us are inclined to help. We want to solve a problem or offer a solution. When you are being an observer for insight purposes, it is important not to jump to a solution because you may not have all the information and context to offer a true improvement over a temporary fix. However, that inclination to help or fix is a strong signal there is a pain point. Make note of this and explore it. What are you observing specifically that requires a solution? What is the benefit of a solution? What other solutions could work? Do these solutions solve any other problems?

Observation skills take time to build. They also require a suspension of judgment. The challenge with ethnography and observation is that the researcher is the data collection instrument. As you are observing and gathering data, you are inherently judging the information to determine what to pay attention to and what to ignore. For this reason, it is helpful to work with a diverse team. Have someone challenge your observations and interpretations because they have different experiences. Observational research is not about seeking consolidation or convergence; it is about exploring.

To conclude this chapter, the Cialis case describes how Eli Lilly and Company applied moments of truth and jobs-to-be-done to connect with patients and partners to distinguish its brand from competitors.

CASE: CIALIS—*"Choosing the Moment"*

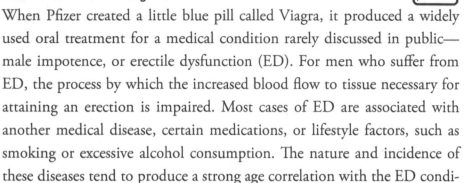

When Pfizer created a little blue pill called Viagra, it produced a widely used oral treatment for a medical condition rarely discussed in public— male impotence, or erectile dysfunction (ED). For men who suffer from ED, the process by which the increased blood flow to tissue necessary for attaining an erection is impaired. Most cases of ED are associated with another medical disease, certain medications, or lifestyle factors, such as smoking or excessive alcohol consumption. The nature and incidence of these diseases tend to produce a strong age correlation with the ED condition. An estimated 30 million men in the United States and 150 million worldwide experience chronic ED. Furthermore, the National Institutes of Health estimates that as many as 52 percent of all men between the ages of forty and seventy experience some form of ED.

Viagra had a notably successful launch. A total of 600,000 prescriptions were filled in the first month (April 1998), and its brand name immediately became the common noun for the symptom it said it would treat—erectile dysfunction. Its recognition far transcended the circles of ED patients. It quickly mushroomed into a cultural phenomenon, becoming the subject of dinner-table conversations and late-night television comedy. Viagra is a prescription medication that has a thirty-minute to one-hour onset time (time from taking the pill until it becomes effective) and requires sexual stimulation for it to produce an erection. Viagra's half-life was three to five hours. Pfizer studies indicated that Viagra improves erection in approximately 80 percent of men who suffer from ED.

It would be five years before the second and third competitors would be approved for use. Levitra was approved in August 2003, with Cialis following close behind in November 2003. Levitra was co-marketed in a joint venture between Bayer Pharmaceuticals with GlaxoSmithKline (GSK) and had a similar time-action profile to Viagra, with effects lasting four hours. Being the first one to market, Viagra focused on fulfilling the physiological unmet need for a man to attain an erection. This would be classified as a "functional" JTBD, based on the description of jobs-to-be-done provided earlier in this chapter. Levitra positioned themselves as not only fulfilling the physiologic need but also emphasized the functional benefit of a quality erection, which, again, would be classified as another "functional" JTBD. David Pernock, senior vice president for marketing at GSK at the time of launch, said, "We give men the quality erections they want."

Lilly had forged a joint venture with ICOS Corporation to co-market Cialis. Even though Cialis would be third to market, the Lilly/ICOS team believed that its thirty-six-hour time-action profile would be a superior product advantage over both Levitra and Viagra, allowing for a longer window for sexual intercourse to happen. However, the challenges for Cialis were many with Viagra's synonymous association with ED, its five years of being tried and tested, and the large competitive direct-to-consumer advertising spends by both Pfizer and GSK that flooded television, radio, magazines, newspapers, and the internet. Of those who prescribed a medication for ED, close to 90 percent said the patient had initiated the request for the drug.

But perhaps the greatest challenge was market research conducted with prescribing physicians revealed that *efficacy* (the fraction of patients for whom the drug would be effective) was the most important attribute, followed by *safety*. These two attributes accounted for a relative importance of roughly 70 percent. The *duration* attribute (indicating how long one dosage of the drug can improve the ability to achieve an erection) was noted by the respondents to have a relative importance of less than 10 percent. The implication was that Cialis (with its thirty-six-hour time-action profile) would have to make duration matter with prescribing physicians. And more importantly, would the longer duration of Cialis be equally valued by all ED patients? Or should the team explore additional jobs-to-be-done for ED beyond just focusing on the functional job of providing a longer duration of action for the male? What other jobs-to-be-done was the team missing that Cialis could solve?

Extensive interviews with both current Viagra users and non-Viagra users revealed in most ED cases, a key moment of truth is when a man first experiences inconsistent ability to perform sexually (physical event). There is a feeling of personal embarrassment (emotional revelation). If the condition persists, another key moment of truth occurs when the individual begins questioning his role in the relationship, accompanied by a sense of unfairness to the female partner; the relationship may become strained (social event). Over time, not only does the ED patient feel insecure and detached from his partner, but this leads to another moment of truth when his self-identity suffers (emotional revelation). This causes him to question his role in other contexts of his life, including his interactions with friends or even colleagues at work. Thus, what started as a relatively noncritical physical condition spirals into a psychological anxiety problem affecting the individual's identity and even his sense of place in the world. Clearly, there appeared to be more associated with ED than a sufferer's inability to attain an erection.

Given most men with ED reported they were in a relationship, market research was also conducted with ED partners, which revealed that partners' satisfaction with Viagra was mixed. Viagra's masculine messages and four-hour window appealed to men but alienated half the target audience: their partners. Virtually all women acknowledged inconveniences with the drug, as reflected in the following statements, which can also be considered key moments of truth from their perspective:

- "My partner must awkwardly ask me if he should take the pill."
- "Once my partner takes the Viagra tablet, I no longer feel I can refuse [to have] sex."
- "Because my partner must ultimately take the tablet, I usually don't initiate sex."
- "It feels like there's three of us in bed—the man, the woman, and the pill."

Most women preferred their male partner take Viagra rather than nothing at all (but a new moment of truth crystallized—when the pill creates pressure rather than connection). After hearing of the potential thirty-six-hour duration of Cialis, men and women described the concept of waiting to "choose the right moment for them" and that "it takes two to tango." As a result, the decision was made to take an alternative approach from Viagra and Levitra by combining the functional job for the male with an emotional and social job for the couple. Instead of trying to beat the giant Viagra with size and power, Cialis would be positioned as support for loving, spontaneous relationships by tying the product's longer duration of action (functional job) to key social and emotional jobs for which the couple was seeking solutions.

Through research and unpacking the moments of truth for both the man and his partner, three key jobs-to-be-done emerged, which informed the core insight for Cialis.

Love and Belonging (Emotional and Social Job)
It's more than just about attaining an erection and performance; it's about being in a loving relationship and feeling that you belong.

Confidence (Functional and Emotional Job)
For the man, he no longer needed to feel embarrassment or anxious. He could now feel confident about consistently performing over a longer period.

Spontaneity (Social Job)
For the couple, it's about restoring and experiencing the spontaneity the relationship once enjoyed before erectile dysfunction—both being ready when the moment is right. This became the core human insight for the launch of Cialis.

Activating the Insight
With this insight in mind, the creative campaign and activation had to do three things:

1. Come from a different direction—a warmer, gentler, and less hurried approach, showing a man and woman side by side in relaxing moments together, in contrast to the male-driven imagery for Viagra and Levitra
2. Continuous presence of women sending the subtle signal that it makes it easier for them to set the pace with their men
3. Keep a certain level of taste by not putting Cialis that close to the sex act (e.g., his-and-her bathtubs rather than a shared hot tub and not a lot of sexual innuendos)
4. Soft look and feel of the campaign using color schemes of pastels, greens, and bright yellow

Cialis debuted its first television ad during the Super Bowl on February 1, 2004. It marked the first time in the Super Bowl's thirty-eight-year history that ads for an ED treatment appeared during the game's telecast. Paced with a soundtrack of laid-back jazz, it unfolded with scenes of couples snuggling and enjoying a tender, playful, or lazy moment, any one of which could turn into the right moment. The settings of these moments range from the extraordinary to the everyday. Couples were seen sharing a relaxing moment watching a coastal sunset, a tender moment in an espresso bar, and a playful moment in the kitchen.

With each couple, the message was clear: with Cialis, there is no need to hurry. *Couples can take their time to choose the moment that is right for them.*

Results

In just three months post-launch, Cialis surpassed Levitra in sales and eventually beat Viagra years later to become the number-one-selling ED treatment worldwide. Cialis continued running this campaign for fourteen years until it lost its patent exclusivity in 2017.

As stated at the beginning of this chapter, what makes pain points difficult is most people can't tell you what they need. The Cialis case is a good example of this principle. By identifying and understanding the essence of the key pain points from the man's and their partner's perspective, it became apparent what the needs were for both involved. This led to the uncovering of a powerful core human insight that Cialis activated successfully throughout its entire lifecycle. Seems easy, right? In reality, this took over a year, and there was intense internal debate for all the reasons discussed in Chapter 2. Organizations, groups, and individuals have their barriers and biases that make this process challenging, even when the end result seems obvious.

Practice: Observation to Moments of Truth to Jobs-to-Be-Done

- **Make the most of the next time you are in waiting—or know you will be waiting.** Consider any situations where you would be waiting, such as at a doctor's office, the pickup line at school, at a restaurant, or in the checkout line at a store. Practice observing the space. Make notes, including a drawing, of the space. What areas are being used? What areas are not being used? What are people saying and doing? Is there an outlier? Is there an inefficiency? Are you inclined to help someone at some point? Why? What would you do or recommend? Why do you think that would help?
- **Observe a setting with meaning to you.** Think about a business or organization that you have a connection to, such as a business owned by a friend or an organization where you are a volunteer. Observe just as above, but this time, after the observation, analyze your notes about pain points using the tools given in this chapter. Identify at least one moment of truth. Now, within that moment of truth, what are the jobs-to-be-done? What might the business or organization do differently because of the moment(s) of truth and job(s)-to-be-done?

CHAPTER 6:
PERSPECTIVES

The other night, I ate at a really nice family restaurant.
Every table had an argument going.
—George Carlin, American comedian

"Let's Get Real"—Mitch

My faith has always been an important part of my life and core to my beliefs, perspectives, and how I view the world. I became a Christian at thirteen years old and have been actively involved in church, leading Bible study groups throughout most of my adult life. I don't pretend to be a scholar of the Bible but just someone who is a lifelong student, who enjoys reading the greatest book ever written and facilitating learning with others. Now, just by these first three sentences, you probably have made some assumptions about me, and possibly a few emotions have bubbled up. I ask you to be aware of that and keep reading.

I recently became involved with a Christian men's ministry called Heart of a Man, which exists to deeply connect men for the purpose of learning, growing, walking through life together, and deepening their Christian faith. Men are not very good at building strong relationships with other men. Heart of a Man is working to address this unspoken need that exists for many men.

I was asked to co-lead a small group of fifteen to twenty men who attend weekly sessions with another man named Jay, who I did not know when we were first assigned as co-leaders. We spoke on the phone to get to know each other a few nights before we were to co-lead our first session together. As we talked, it quickly became apparent that we were different men who came from very different backgrounds. I was a white male who grew up in the rural South, in a conservative, traditional home with a mother and father. I went to college and became a pharmacist. Jay is a Black male and grew up on the streets in the inner city of Detroit without a father; he did not attend college. He owns and manages a successful pawn shop in Indianapolis. Needless to say, except for our Christian faith, many of our perspectives and views of the world differ. However, I have come to discover and appreciate Jay's perspectives and views as a result of his culture and upbringing that I otherwise would have never known or experienced. I have learned to be a better listener and challenge my conventional thinking—in a positive way—because of Jay.

Some men feel uncomfortable sharing in a group setting. It's imperative that a leader be sensitive but also active in drawing men out. As a result of growing up in the inner-city of Detroit, Jay is good at exploring what men are saying or not saying and drawing them out in a sensitive way. One of Jay's catchphrases is "Let's get real."

As leaders, one of our responsibilities is to call each man in our groups every week to connect with them individually outside the group. I remember after the first week, one of the men I called commented (voluntarily) to me, "You and Jay could not be more different, but it works for the group because you can use each other's diverse backgrounds to explore deeper and richer perspectives of the Christian faith for the benefit of the group." That confirmed for me that being paired with a co-leader who does not necessarily have the same perspectives or views as I do was far better than being paired with someone just like me. The conversations and the learnings within the group have been far richer and more diverse as a result. And more importantly, Jay has become a close friend whom I never would have intentionally made on my own.

Melinda and I have been working together for several years as business partners. We are similar in some ways, but like Jay, we have different perspectives. We don't agree on everything, but we listen, debate, respect, and, most importantly, value uncovering each other's perspectives. As a result, we have a strong working relationship because we can challenge, push each other's thinking, and avoid judging each other. I recently told

Melinda she knew me better than any of my other work colleagues—even those I have known for decades. I believe this is a result of our insights work together. We practice what we preach.

Importance of Gaining Different Perspectives

Chances are you already made a judgment about someone today. Generally, judgment happens when someone's behavior or beliefs are not consistent with either your own or the way you think or want that person to behave. Remaining in our own shoes to interpret someone else's world means we will never understand another's perspective. Rather, we will be stuck in our own judgment, assumptions, and biases.

It used to be an unspoken rule that there are two topics people should not discuss—religion and politics—because they are personal and can foster disagreement, even hostility between people. Today, politics has infiltrated our lives in many ways, and a deep polarization has emerged within society. Destroying the other side has become the goal. There are many causes for this polarization, including demographic changes, political ideology, social and mass media, and more. But perhaps the biggest contributor to the polarization is people's unwillingness to take the time to listen and seek to understand others' perspectives and beliefs that may be different from our own.

We call our third pillar for insights "perspectives" because to truly understand another person you must shift from the filter of your experience and background—your perspective—and see the world from the other person, from their perspective. Making this perspective shift will not only enable insight discovery, but it gives us a better understanding and greater empathy for others, whether it be a spouse, child, parent, friend, co-worker, customer, or even an adversary. It reduces bias, judgment, and conflict. Perhaps the greatest benefit of gaining perspectives is opening the opportunity to new relationships that can become deeply meaningful in your life.

Taking time to see things from other perspectives allows us to:	. . . and the benefit is:
See a problem or challenge from different angles to develop a better solution	Gaining greater clarity
Re-evaluate the importance of something	Personal growth
Abate worries or thoughts	Reducing stress
Let go of judgment and focus on facts	Learning opportunities
See the new strengths and weaknesses/good and bad/positive and negative	Developing deeper empathy
React rationally and considerately rather than impulsively	Responding constructively not impulsively
Become aware of our bias	Avoiding judgment

Thinking Human First

It may sound cliché, but to really understand another's perspective to uncover meaningful insights, we must first take on a human-centric mindset and approach.

Human-centricity means thinking of others as human first, not as their relationship to you—like customer, teammate, or constituent— but framing your understanding by thinking of them as a human being first. Think of this as your initial port of entry into understanding. A human-centric approach asks you to understand others' needs from their point of view to enable empathy. An empathetic approach means we step into their experience and environment and become one with them. This is often hard for us since it's so tempting to think about our experiences and layer them on others. For example, we may think we know what it is like to have chronic back pain because we had a back problem for a couple of weeks in the past, but we don't know what it is like to have the pain for the rest of our lives and the impact it has on our psyche.

Something that works against us in having a human-centric mindset is the idea, "I know me, so I know them." The assumption is that their experience base is consistent with ours. An easy way to identify this assumption is when you are offered unsolicited advice that is well-intended but not helpful. This could be a new grandparent giving advice to the new parent—their child—about how to raise their new grandchild. It could also be the parents of a bride or groom offering their advice to the newlyweds. Whatever the scenario, the advice comes from someone who believes they have similar experiences but misses the differences of time, context, and, of course, the other person's perspectives.

We like to emphasize to teams we work with that no matter how long you have worked in the field, category, or industry, you can never know enough about the depths of the beliefs, attitudes, motivations, emotions, and feelings your end-users are experiencing. To avoid becoming complacent and ego-centric in your thinking, the assumption should always be that you are still many steps away from completely understanding a specific individual or target customer. There is always more to learn.

We also fail to recognize the distance created between us and others. A. G. Lafley, when he was the CEO at Proctor & Gamble, went into the homes of average Americans a couple times of a month. In a *Forbes* story published in 2002, Lafley explained at the time, "Executives in the United States were buried under consumer research data. I don't think the answers are just in the numbers. You have to get out and look." This is why he constantly visited homes and stores. This practice carried forward as we discussed in the Febreze case in Chapter 3.

Thinking with a "human first" mindset is challenging. It takes practice, patience, and reflection—all of which are challenged by our busy schedules, pressing timelines, and purpose for our insight discovery. We start with good intentions, but it is easy for our perspective to slip back in as a shortcut. The rest of this chapter will provide self-guided tools to help keep your perspective from creeping in as you try to understand others.

How to Get at Perspectives

1. Seeing how others experience the world

The ability to see and feel how others experience the world is called empathetic intuition. Before we get too deep into empathy, we need to make an important distinction. Empathy says, "I feel your state," and that by stepping into your shoes, I can understand and feel you from your perspective. Sympathy is feeling pity or sorrow for someone or something. Pity keeps you at a distance from others. It risks a feeling of disconnect.

Empathy leads to trust. We don't trust people we don't have a feeling for. Think about that in the context of relationships. If others don't feel we understand them, they won't trust us. Empathy doesn't involve crying or heartbreak—at least not necessarily—but seeing and feeling as if we were them. Our goal is empathy, not sympathy. An important starting point is that we all have an innate ability, a gut sense—in fact, a biological ability—for feeling the experiences of others. We are wired to think this way, yet the pressure of time and commitments steer us more toward sympathy than empathy.

2. Feelings vs. emotions

How we perceive the world largely depends on our emotions. Emotions influence how we live and interact with each other. The choices we make, the actions we take, and the perceptions we have are all influenced by the emotions we experience at any given moment. The emotions we feel have a subjective, physiological, and expressive component—how we experience the emotion and how our body reacts to the emotion can influence the actions we take and the decisions we make to help us survive, avoid danger, form social connections, and thrive.

Many people use the terms "feeling" and "emotion" as synonyms, but they are not interchangeable. While they have similar elements, there is a marked difference between feelings and emotions.

Feelings. Both emotional experiences and physical sensations—such as hunger or pain—bring about feelings. Feelings are a conscious experience.

Emotions. An emotion "can only ever be felt . . . through the emotional experiences it gives rise to, even though it might be discovered through its associated thoughts, beliefs, desires, and actions." Emotions are not conscious but instead manifest in the unconscious mind.

A fundamental difference between feelings and emotions is that feelings are experienced consciously, while emotions manifest either consciously or subconsciously. Some people may spend years, or even a lifetime, not understanding the depths of their emotions.

As mentioned earlier in Chapter 1, in our experience, when insights don't have an emotional component, then they usually do not reach the bar we set for an insight. Emotions can help us dig deeper to understand the *why* behind the behavior. Further, just like an insight, emotions are enduring over time—more so than tangible needs and functional benefits. The challenge is uncovering these emotions when they are likely not fully aware or understood by the other person. Fortunately, we have tools and frameworks we can apply to better understand.

Making Sense of Others' Feelings and Emotions

Throughout life, humans experience many emotions. This range of emotions is impacted by such factors as their behavior, the culture they come from, who their parents are, where they grew up, where they went to school, and their previous traumatic experiences.

A 2015 research paper published in *Harvard Business Review,* called "The New Science of Customer Emotions," demonstrates that when companies connect with customers' emotions, the payoff can be huge. Scott Magids, Alan Zorfas, and Daniel Leemon's research across hundreds of brands in dozens of categories show it is possible to rigorously measure and strategically target the feelings and emotions that drive customer behavior. They find customers become more valuable at each step of a predictable "emotional connection pathway" as they transition from (1) being uncon-nected to (2) being highly satisfied to (3) perceiving brand differentiation to (4) being fully connected. Although customers exhibit increasing con-nection at each step, their value increases dramatically when they reach the fourth step: Fully connected customers are 52 percent more valuable, on average, than those who are just highly satisfied.

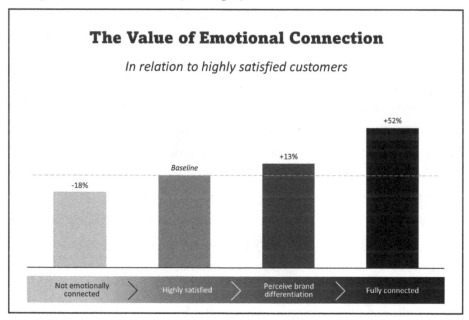

When we work with teams in uncovering the emotions that may be driving the *why* behind the behavior, the goal is to move beyond the superficial level. Most of our work is in the healthcare and pharmaceutical spaces. There is nothing more emotional than our health. For example, someone being told they have cancer for the first time is a very emotional experience. They feel a range of emotions, from sadness to fear to anger. Our oncology clients provide medications and experiences that tend to focus on the promise of hope. After all, isn't hope what a person with cancer wants most—whether it is grounded in surviving an early death or being able to live in remission? However, there are many ways to describe and express the emotion of hope that may convey a deeper meaning or do a better job of connecting with how a person living with cancer wants to feel. We encourage teams to get beyond the foundational or superficial level of hope, especially if there are many treatment regimens that are all promising hope too.

It is estimated there are over 34,000 distinguishable combinations of emotions. Through years of studying emotions, psychologist Robert Plutchik proposed eight primary emotions that serve as the foundation for all others: joy, sadness, acceptance, disgust, fear, anger, surprise, and anticipation. Below is an adaptation of Plutchik's Wheel of Emotions. There are many other emotion wheels available; however, this is the one we find more useful.

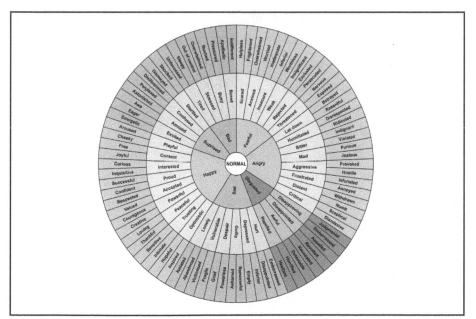

How They Want to Feel

As pointed out earlier, strong brands connect not only on a rational or functional level but also on an emotional level. Typically, when we're working with a client, we will get to a point or a stage of development where it's obvious the team needs to move beyond focusing solely on the rational and functional benefits and start thinking about how to connect what the brand offers to customers' emotions in a meaningful way. Many teams we work with will have completed a customer journey to identify what a particular segment of people are currently doing and feeling at each stage of their journey (described in Chapter 5). However, the goal is not to simply answer how they *currently* feel at any one stage of their journey but also how they *want to* feel.

Graeme Newell, a behavioral researcher and emotional marketing expert, says your typical marketing campaign starts by identifying a product feature, but good emotional marketing doesn't start with the product. It starts with how the customer wants to feel about themselves and then the product feature demonstrates that feeling. Think about a recent effective advertisement you saw that grabbed your attention. Most likely, the advertisement led with a need and how you want to feel, then the product was revealed, demonstrating how it would help you feel that way. In all of Newell's video case examples, he plays this cadence of setting up the emotional connection first, then bringing in the brand. One of our favorite examples he uses is a commercial for V8 juice. It starts by showing this woman waterskiing. You have no idea how old she is until they zoom in on her and show a visual that states she's an eighty-three-year-old professional waterskier. And then, of course, she starts drinking her V8 juice. She's healthy. It's healthy. We know all the rational benefits of tomato juice, but they are connecting it to how the customer wants to feel, which is young and energetic. It's a very real, authentic connection of emotion to the brand benefits.

How the COPD Patient Wants to Feel

Let's go back to our COPD example. In Chapter 5, we provided an example of a patient journey. Here, we learned patients take time to make the connection between their symptoms and smoking history and the eventual COPD diagnosis. For the physician, this is not the case. They suspect COPD earlier on in the journey, based on the onset of symptoms and smoking history. When the patient is finally made aware of their diagnosis, we called this phase of their journey "shock and shame." Clearly, we have identified feelings and emotions, but how do they *want* to feel?

Uncovering how people want to feel is layered. First, you need to step into their shoes to empathize and identify their true emotions. Next, you have to step outside of this emotion to see it from another angle, which they cannot see themselves. You have to make an assumption to determine how they want to feel. This assumption will be more accurate the more you can empathize with the other person.

A published qualitative study among patients diagnosed with COPD, who already had other comorbidities, offered further context to the "shock and shame" phase. The researchers concluded patients tended to be resigned toward accepting their COPD diagnosis and were passive. Why would they feel this way? Think about the last time you felt resigned or passive to something really important in your life. Is it because you didn't care? Probably not. It is more likely to be something you care a great deal about, but it was out of your control. If you were just told you had COPD—a condition with no cure that will slowly decrease your ability to breathe—and it was likely because of your smoking history, which you can't change, you would likely feel out of control too.

Another great source we found to better understand the COPD sufferer was a letter to the editor of the journal of the COPD Foundation. Here is an excerpt from that letter:

We have new hope, new stunning data, [and] new provocative results from a landmark clinical trial of over 10,000 COPD patients with a smoking history, funded by the National Institutes of Health (NIH) since 2008. The principal investigators looked deep into our genes and now propose new ways to define and diagnose COPD. We are facing hope that current and future interventions can slow and ultimately stop COPD progression before disability or irreversible lung structural changes develop. The framework—exposures (here cigarette smoking), spirometry (forced expiratory volume in 1 second), symptoms (dyspnea, exacerbations), computed tomography imaging (structural lung abnormalities)—support a new formula allowing a re-examination of how COPD patients might be identified earlier, treated earlier and classified ultimately by phenotype. We are not all the same.

Clearly, there is a desire to feel hopeful about the future of COPD—but what else do you read in the letter? *We are not all the same.* These six words speak volumes. COPD patients want to be seen and their condition validated by being included within the scientific community as an area of focus and innovation. One of our favorite examples of pulling through how patients want to feel (beyond hopeful) is for a product called Kisqali (a treatment for HR+/HER2- metastatic breast cancer). In their advertising and on their website, they use the statement, "We want science, not sorrys." When we first heard this line, we knew this brand had a deep understanding of how a woman with breast cancer wants to feel.

Looking outside your category is another tool we can use within the perspectives pillar. Emotions are not unique to one condition; they are core to who we are as humans. We can get ideas and hypotheses by looking at other situations or categories that elicit the same emotional response to aid our hypothesis for how they want to feel.

Critical Skill: Active Listening

I never learned anything while I was talking.
—Larry King, American TV and radio host

As supported by a 2015 study evaluating the learning goals of accredited undergraduate business schools, a formal curriculum is concentrated on speaking rather than listening. In this study, 78 percent of the universities had a learning goal focused on presenting, while only 11 percent had a goal on listening. For this reason, we prioritized the critical skill in this chapter on how to be a better listener. There are several articles offering guidance and tips, but as with any skill, these will only improve your ability to a certain level. To truly become a better listener, you must practice doing it. Here, we offer a few key principles and tips that can help you to become a better listener.

Minimize distractions. Most of us know eye contact is important, whether we are speaking or listening. We might not be aware of all the distractions that cause us to break eye contact as well as our focus. Our most common are digital devices, such as laptops and phones, but here are some others that might be less obvious: a smartwatch vibration, nearby sounds (such as a timer in a kitchen or breakroom), and foot traffic of coworkers/co-inhabitants in your space. For these reasons, it is important to not only shut off devices but also consider finding a location that has fewer distractions and/or using a "do not disturb" sign whenever possible.

Repeat and summarize. Saying back what you have heard does two things in a conversation: 1) confirms the information, and 2) gives the speaker encouragement and recognition that they are being heard. Do not "put it in your own words," which will have the opposite effect. Repeating and summarizing in the speaker's words will help you stay focused and pay attention. Only "put in your own words" when you need clarification; otherwise, this phrase can signal the conversation is shifting to your point of view rather than staying in the speaker's.

Consider applying the following tip: Visualize what the speaker is saying in your mind rather than writing notes. This will help you retain the intent and emotion of what you are hearing. It will also help you stay engaged and relay back what you have heard.

Monitor Non-verbals. Look for body language to match or run counter to the words being said. Is the person saying, "It was fine" but sitting with their arms crossed? These disconnections in verbal and non-verbal language might direct you to new questions. For example, if your guest says dinner was "fine" but the person scrunches up their nose, a follow-up question would be, "Was there any part that could be improved?"

Your non-verbals are equally important to monitor. Even though you should be speaking less, you are saying plenty by how you sit and with your eye contact and facial expressions. Be mindful that you want to use all of these to encourage the speaker to tell you more.

Listen to Learn. It might seem obvious, but remind yourself you are listening to learn. This means you need to monitor your emotions and quiet your agenda. The person you are listening to might say something you disagree with or run counter to something you feel passionate about. First, it is critical that you become aware of your emotional response. This means you are much more likely to listen less or selectively listen because you are formulating the counterargument. The best approach is to slow the pace of the conversation because speeding up your speech will signal tension. Think of simple, open-ended questions to ask or default to, "Could you tell me more about that?"

Use your emotional response as a signal that you are about to learn something new and reframe it as a positive. Hal Gregersen, executive director of the MIT Leadership Center, suggests, "We need information that is disconfirming, not confirming. If we ever finish a conversation and learned nothing surprising, we weren't really listening."

Monitor Your Talk:Listen Ratio. This tip is more helpful in group discussions. Draw a map or chart of everyone involved in the conversation and make hash marks every time someone talks (including yourself). This will help monitor the participation of the group. Sometimes it is obvious who is dominant in a group. Other times, we identify people who use more words than others but, in reality, are participating in an equal/fair amount.

Even if you are having a one-on-one conversation with someone, monitoring can be helpful—especially if you are known to talk more than listen. Make a goal to ask more questions than make statements. Monitoring this dynamic will also help you stay engaged in the conversation.

Don't Interrupt. Some people take longer to formulate their thoughts into words than others. Be mindful that interrupting someone signals a power dynamic even when it is not intentional. If you think the person is done speaking ask, "Are you ready to move on to another topic?" This is also a good time to repeat and summarize what you have heard. This can help the speaker add to their thoughts if they were struggling to find their words.

Asking questions is also a critical skill tied to listening. In fact, we believe asking questions is its own skill and will be described further in the next chapter.

Now, let's look at a specific case example of when the emotions of how second-time moms wanted to feel led to a powerful insight that Luvs leveraged to connect successfully with its end-users.

CASE: LUVS DISPOSABLE DIAPERS— *"Second-Time Moms and the Truth about Parenting"*

When we teach insights, Luvs, the disposable diaper, is a favorite example of ours. Luvs is made by Procter & Gamble. Initially, Luvs were sold as "deluxe" diapers in the late 1980s. After launch, Luvs ranked a distant fourth in terms of value share within the US diaper category at 8.9 percent. Pampers and Huggies were both premium-priced diapers that made up most of the category, with value share at 31 percent and 41 percent, respectively. Private Label was the third biggest player, with 19 percent of the value share. The challenge for Procter and Gamble was they needed to generate awareness to drive trial for Luvs to grow the brand, but a few things stood in their way: low share of voice, negative quality perception, and the competition owned the emotions of joy and the magic of newborn babies. Both Pampers and Huggies both laid claim to these emotions.

The key was not to explore babies—Huggies and Pampers advertising had this down to a tee—but to switch the focus to moms. It was found that even amid the joys of babies, there is a lot of anxiety and guilt that comes with being a new mom. Tons of books, magazines, and blogs are written spouting advice on what to do and what not to do. What's the "right" way to parent? Are you following the rules correctly? Are you doing the "best" for your baby? New moms, unused to their new bundles of joy, relied on these sources to tell them how to do things the "right" way. They felt a tremendous amount of responsibility to live up to their high standards and wanted, more than anything, to give their babies the very best. Unsurprisingly, Huggies and Pampers more than answered this need, providing a high-premium offering and a deep understanding of the magic babies bring. But in talking to moms, they noticed this emotion wasn't shared by everybody. The tone and mood shifted when they spoke to moms who had one thing in common—their second (or third or fourth) child.

The anxiety of doing things "the right way" was something experienced moms no longer bought into. The need to be perfect was not something they cared about, mostly because they knew this idea was unattainable and not realistic. They were tired of being told what was "best." They talked of "trial and error" and the importance of experience. These moms felt their take on parenting was not reflected by baby brand advertising. A lot of it felt too perfect. They still liked seeing their babies' world brought to life through advertising, but they didn't see themselves represented.

What's more, there was a business case for this audience: Nielsen data showed Luvs over-indexed with experienced moms. And it answered the need to prove quality. Who better to vouch for the efficacy of the product than a seen-it-all-before mom who simply wants to get the job done quickly and effectively? As a result, the decision was made to make Luvs the official diaper of multiple-children moms. Luvs alone would champion *experienced* moms.

Insights into the experienced mom would be vital to connecting with this segment. Through research, three key themes emerged that informed the tone of the work.

1. *Confidence*
   She trusts her instincts and doesn't sway in the face of external pressures to be a perfect mom. She makes no apologies.

2. *Humor*
   She laughs at herself. She knows she'll make mistakes and is now more apt to laugh than cry.

3. *Honesty*
   She's not ashamed to admit that sometimes it's not always pretty, but she's figured out what works for her and her baby—and she's not afraid to admit it. No judgments. With time and experience, she's figured out that there's no such thing as perfect parenting. Loving your kids and getting by in a way that was right for you is all that matters. Although, what she tells no one else is she is seeking validation that her way is okay.

A consistent pattern emerged and was heard in the stories experienced moms told, which contrasted their parental techniques with their first baby against their techniques with their second or third child.

- When first babies fall over or fall off the bed, moms go to the Emergency Room. When second babies fall over, moms pick them up, dust them down, and get on with the cleaning.

- When first babies go to sleep, the mom sits nervously over the child intercom, listening to them, waiting for them to wake up. When second babies go to sleep, the wine bottle is uncorked two minutes later. One mom said, "Bedtime is at 8:00 p.m. Mommy Happy Hour starts at 8:02 p.m."
- When first babies need a story, they get a children's book. When second babies need a story, they get *Fifty Shades of Grey*. "My baby won't know the difference," we were told, "and it's much more fun for me."

With these statements in mind, the creative execution had to do three things:

1. Tonally play to the attitude of moms being funny, honest, and unapologetic
2. Actively play up the difference between first- and second-time moms, validating their way is okay—if not smarter
3. Spark as much debate as possible

The construct of the creative campaign was brilliant in the way it showed a mom evolving from her first kid to her second. In so doing, she goes from being inexperienced to an expert. From a ball of stress to cool and calm under pressure. From awkward to unapologetic.

The copywriting beautifully summed up the insight: "By their second kid, every mom is an expert and more likely to choose Luvs. Live, Learn and Get Luvs."

In just one year, Luvs increased its share of the market from 8.9 percent to 9.6 percent, the biggest increase and highest share in the brand's history. What's more, such a share increase was worth a huge $38 million. Luvs has continued running this campaign for over ten years now, showing how uncovering and owning a core human insight for a specific target customer can lead to success for many years.

Practice: Get to Know Your Strangers

- **The next time you are sitting next to a stranger, immerse yourself in their story**
  When you talk with other people, make a conscious effort to work on your listening skills. Monitor your emotions to ensure you are capturing their perspective rather than working on your counterargument when you disagree with their perspective. Your goal should be to learn at least one new thing from this person, and they should leave the conversation feeling heard and seen rather than defensive.

- **Think about how you would feel in another person's situation**
  If you meet or hear about someone who has experienced hardship, imagine how you would feel in that person's situation as a way to build empathy for them and gain a new perspective. How might you feel if you had gone through a similar experience? Why might you feel that way? What might you do to cope with the experience?

- **Go somewhere outside your comfort zone**
  Try attending a religious service at a church, synagogue, mosque, or another place of worship in your community that will present beliefs that differ from yours. Another option is to visit a restaurant in a vastly different part of your city.

CHAPTER 7:
PERPLEXITIES

*I think comedy is an angry art form; it's an outsider art form.
Anger and comedy are really connected. If I'm angry about
something I will try to think about something funny about it
to lighten the load of the anger and cope with the anger.*
—Margaret Cho, American comedian and actress

"No One Likes to Be Wrong"—Melinda

Every Fourth of July, my family gets together at our house to celebrate. This involves seven to ten days filled with an obscene amount of fireworks explosions, meat consumption, cocktails, sun exposure, and swearing. We end the celebration with hugs, declarations to get in better shape, recommendations to "dry out," and a general understanding that next year we will do it all over again.

There are few rules over the Fourth holiday. These rules only exist to make sure we want to see each other the next year. The main rule is that certain topics are off-limits. If you bring them up, you have to do a shot. Most years, we uncover a new topic we should avoid. The year 2022 was no exception. We all assumed the landmark court decision to overturn *Roe vs. Wade* would be the taboo topic to avoid circumventing words we couldn't take back—but no. It turned out to be which of my brothers would win in a car race.

To put this argument into context, my older brother races a Miata as a hobby. My younger brother was looking to buy a sports car. Somehow, the topic trended to which car would be the fastest in a road race. Voices got louder. Children got worried. Most of us decided it was time to go to bed.

Family get-togethers are excellent opportunities to witness one of my favorite insights play out: no one likes to be wrong. How often have we seen someone (or experienced it ourselves) when the realization they could possibly be wrong pops into their mind and they squash it down? Perhaps, as with me, you know this is happening to you because your face starts to change color or your voice gets louder. In the case of my brothers, swear words replaced everyday words until they dominated entire sentences.

In our personal lives, this insight is important because it can cause us to do or say things we regret. As a marketer, this insight is important because our customers don't want to be put on the defensive. Prior decisions, behaviors, and overindulgences can feel confrontational. For this reason, it is important we recognize when we are pushing against someone's belief system, and additional force is a waste of energy.

Jonah Berger describes this in the first chapter of his book, *The Catalyst How to Change Anyone's Mind*. Specifically, he talks about the efforts to curb illegal or unhealthy behavior, which is often met with resistance. "Telling people not to do something has the opposite effect: it makes them more likely to do it."

Personally, when I come across a tense scenario, triggered by opposite views and those who believe they are right, my default is humor. I try to break the tension with laughter and then try to find common ground (I am a middle child, after all). In my professional life, I have to take a different approach.

Marketers often have blinders on when it comes to their products. I see red flags when I hear, "The product will sell itself," only to later lament over their customers who "just didn't understand the data." We struggle to recognize our customers' barriers because we love our products. Our goal as marketers is to change behavior, and that often requires changing people's minds. More messages to reinforce your selling points only encourage those who already bought in. Convincing someone on the other side requires a different approach.

We have already mentioned the importance of debate in insight discovery. This is easier said than done. Debate means conflict, and conflict means discomfort. While I still hate to be wrong, I try to remind myself of times when those close to me were right. I'm working on more often saying the phrase, "You were right" and "I was completely wrong about that one." These are important tools for embracing the debate and making it advantageous. To us, the most important skill within the debate is to embrace the disconnects, or what we will call in this book, *perplexities.*

I Don't Know about That

"I don't know about that" has become a favorite phrase in our office and working group. It is a fun way to say you don't believe something to be true. Whenever we are reviewing data as part of insight discovery, we can count on someone from the team to say, "I don't know about that." Or, at least we hope someone says this.

Perplexities are simple enough to define; ***the state of having conflicting data points or perspectives***. The challenge is how to manage perplexities when they are revealed. Anyone who regularly presents data to a group has likely had an audience member challenge the presentation with conflicting data. It feels like an attack, and our instinct is to defend our data. But this is not the right approach. We have learned to embrace this occurrence rather than be challenged by it. As humans, we have an expectation for data to align and assimilate to form consistent and reliable facts about the world. As an insight explorer, we seek the opposite. Whenever we see two or more data points that seem accurate but lead to different conclusions, we get excited. It suggests there is new learning we need to uncover—the cause for the perplexity.

Which One Is Right?

Perhaps stemming from our insight, *no one likes to be wrong*, we often see teams start with this question when they have perplexing data: "Which one is right?" We acknowledge that asking *which one is right* is a fair question. In our insight classes, we instruct participants who may have conflicting data points to assume they are both right in the interest of time. However, we should start with a proper investigation of the data points to validate our confidence that we can trust the sources and facilitate our insight discovery.

Investigating and validating a data point should include three core components: **Who** reported the data, by **how many,** and with **what instruction?**

Let's start with an example from COPD to dive into the *who, how many,* and *with what instruction.* In Chapter 4, we shared the following results of a quantitative study: *Researchers found among adult patients with known risk factors for COPD and who were actively under the care of a physician that about one in five met the criteria for a formal diagnosis of COPD. Among those patients, only one in three was aware of this possible diagnosis.*

Let's suppose you were presenting this data and an audience member says, "But the Center for Disease Control [CDC] estimates that closer to 50 percent of patients that meet the criteria for COPD are undiagnosed. This data suggests it is 66 percent. What is the right answer, one in two or two in three?" Following up on this question, you first track down the sources for the CDC undiagnosed COPD statistic, and you find the following: *Rates range from 12 to 72 percent,* depending on the study and approach. The perplexity is even greater than you thought.

In the first study, which was published in a reputable medical journal, the source were patients in a primary care office. They were included because of their history, given tests to confirm the diagnosis, and then asked if they were ever told they had COPD. After screening for having the correct criteria and agreeing to participate, the sample size is 205 patients. Among them, sixty-seven were unaware of their diagnosis. This is how we got only one in three were aware of their diagnosis and assume two in three were undiagnosed.

In the CDC reports, the ranges come from epidemiology studies where the intent is to measure prevalence. Their sample sizes are much larger, and the patients are recruited to represent a nationally projectable sample. While they had a wide range provided, further reading uncovered that it is because they applied multiple-diagnosis criteria. The most accepted criteria based on history and multiple tests resulted in 50 percent.

Let's get back to the "which is right" question. You could argue the 50 percent is most accurate because it represents a projectable sample of patients. But did the 66 percent really measure the undiagnosed rate—or the unawareness rate? Both statistics provide important information about this market. Rather than throw out the 66 percent, what do both statistics tell us about the market? Here are a few conclusions and new questions you could arrive at:

- COPD underdiagnosis is a problem in the market
- Patients are often unaware of their diagnosis—is it because of a lack of communication from the physician? Is it formally or informally written in the chart?
- Criteria to diagnose COPD results have a wide range of prevalence; which is most applied in the physician's office?

The Framing Effect

Another source of perplexities in data is when we fail to recognize the impact wording has on our responses. Market researchers are typically given training to look for order bias in surveys but not the impact of framing bias on potential results. *Framing, or the framing effect, simply refers to our preference for positive wording over negative wording and* has been shown to have a significant impact on how we answer questions. Again, taking an example from health care, we often assume physicians to be rational and less susceptible to the impact of positive or negative wording—and yet we find a significant difference in how they evaluate a product when shown the same data point framed in two different ways. Take the following example, which split physicians into two groups to review a product profile for a hypothetical asthma drug. Everything was the same, except the following wording:

Group 1: 95% of patients were not hospitalized with exacerbations during the first month of therapy.

Group 2: 5% of patients were hospitalized with exacerbations during the first month of therapy.

(Note: Exacerbation for those non-medical readers means a worsening of symptoms.)

Based on this setup, you can probably guess the results are different, but how much different? In this study, physicians rated their enthusiasm for adopting the new medicine on a scale from 1 to 10. Here are their average scores:

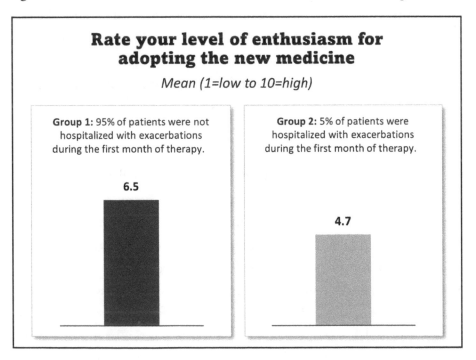

The difference between the two groups is statistically significant. Group 1 received what would be called a positive frame, while Group 2 received a negative frame. "95%" and "not hospitalized" imply something better than "5%" and "hospitalized." Rationally, you can look at both statements and see they are the same, but these physicians only saw one statement, which shows the impact of the wording alone.

Framing is important in perplexities because the way we ask a question and the way we frame it can result in different answers. It does not mean one is right and the other is wrong. It means there is learning when we accept they are both right and look for the explanation of how. In this example, physicians gravitate toward positive framing of data. This is also why our critical skill for this chapter is how to ask a great question.

Tension Points

We briefly mentioned tensions as something to be represented in customer journey mapping in Chapter 5. *Tensions are when two important groups or stakeholders view something differently, and it impedes progress or creates an impasse.* Tensions are common occurrences when we talk about perplexities because those groups will often represent conflicting data or views. Like other perplexities, these tensions should be embraced and explored because they often signal an insight.

Looking at the COPD example again, in an international survey of physicians and patients, 78 percent of physicians strongly agreed, "smoking is the cause of most cases of COPD," while only 38 percent of patients strongly agreed. This represents tension because patients and physicians view smoking as the cause of COPD differently. The *why* is likely tied to the insight at the beginning of this chapter: "No one likes to be wrong."

At this point, we have shared several interesting data points about COPD. Tension points can help connect the dots between some of these discoveries—which we will cover in more detail in the final section. Think about this tension and the other data. What hypotheses do you have? What questions do you have? Could this tension point be impacting the progress of the patient, such as getting a formal diagnosis? Are physicians reluctant to tell patients they have COPD because they know patients do not want to be blamed for their smoking history?

As we say in every class where we bring up tensions, these are neither bad nor good. They might be known to both parties, known to only one of the parties, or unknown to both. Tension can also exist between a person and a thing. In Chapter 5, the Cialis case shared quotes that represented tension between the female partner and Viagra ("the pill"). Once you uncover the tension, your next step is to figure out why it is impeding progress or creating an impasse. In the case of Cialis, "the pill" represented pressure and a loss of spontaneity. In COPD, the patient's smoking history could represent shame and blame, which prevents specific conversations about their condition.

Perplexities within Ourselves

So far, we have represented perplexities as sourced from different places, but it is also possible to have a perplexity within ourselves. When we see this in others, we immediately navigate toward a negative tone and view it as hypocritical. Insight discovery is not about judgment but looking for the *why*. When you recognize your group of interest has a viewpoint you would refer to as hypocritical, use it as a signal to dive deeper and look for an insight. What is the explanation that allows someone to think one way in a scenario or topic and then have the opposite view in a new scenario or topic?

The truth is, we are rarely 100 percent in agreement on something. There are always degrees of agreement with something and recognition that there are situations where we disagree. Parts Therapy is an approach sometimes taken with a trained therapist to uncover the different "parts of yourself" to deal with trauma or other psychological concerns. This approach is effective because it allows people to be more than one thing. You can both love and dislike your sibling, for example. This approach is adapted by some trained professionals in market research settings to get a better understanding of those internal perplexities we have. For example, a consumer can be cost-conscious when shopping for some items and then frivolous in other shopping scenarios. Assuming you are not "playing therapist," an effective tool is to phrase a question like, "What part of you feels this way?" followed by "Is there a part of you that feels the opposite at times?"

Recognizing people have these internal perplexities allows for a richer understanding of who they are and why they might do things counter to what they say. A great example of this is the case of the Dove Real Beauty campaign.

In the early 2000s, Dove was looking for a way to revive its brand. As part of the research to determine their approach, an international survey with more than 3,000 women found several internal perplexities women have about beauty. The two data points that stood out to Dove were:

- 85 percent of women agree with "every woman has something about her that is beautiful"
- Only 2 percent of women considered themselves beautiful

Dove recognized this opportunity to connect with women and start a conversation about beauty. Their Real Beauty Campaign sought to celebrate natural physical differences in women to encourage confidence and happiness with themselves. Not only has this campaign been a success in terms of sales, but a Harvard psychologist, Nancy Etcoff, has found the campaign has impacted the way women describe beauty using a wide range of qualities, including those that are not physical.

As stated earlier, we believe a critical skill to help with understanding perplexities is how we ask questions. So let's look at how we can ask—not just better questions, but—great ones.

Critical Skills: Asking a Great Question

In a *Harvard Business Review* article called, "The Surprising Power of Questions," the authors ask a simple question: *why?* Why do we ask questions? Research has shown there is an obvious reason—to learn something—and a less obvious reason—to impress the person you are asking or someone else within earshot.

Ask questions the other person will enjoy answering. (Dale Carnegie)

In insight discovery, we have two purposes for asking questions as well. The first is the same—to learn more about the person we are directing the question to—and the second is to facilitate discussion. Asking questions is an art form, and like listening, it requires focus and practice. The following are tips to help perfect the art of asking a great question.

Ask Open-Ended Questions

The best place to start for improving your questioning skills is to prioritize open-ended questions over closed-ended questions. Think about your recent conversation with a loved one. You might have asked about their day. Here is a good/better/best approach to asking that question.

Good: *How was your day?* This is how most of us would ask the question. With a loved one, they are likely to elaborate with more than an "okay" or "fine" response—unless you are asking your teenager. This, however, is a closed-ended question because it can be answered with one word.

Better: *Tell me about your day.* Technically, this is a demand and not a question, but it is how we often start when we are asking open-ended questions and trying to avoid the one-word response. The question is implied.

Best: *What was the highlight of your day today?* This question is the best for a few reasons. Not only does the person have to answer in more than one word (open-ended), but they will likely enjoy answering it, which brings us to our next tip.

It's Not about You

As mentioned before, sometimes we ask questions to make ourselves look smart. In insight discovery, our goal is for the person we are asking to feel smart and important. We are not looking for the "gotcha" question, which is why we place this skill in perplexities. If we are asking a question to get a deeper understanding of why they think something—and perhaps also think the opposite because of an internal perplexity—we must create a safe answering environment.

A great place to start is to jot down questions you enjoy answering. Once you have those questions, practice asking them with others. We have a colleague who is the best at this. Every conversation you have with him leaves you feeling heard, smart, and important. You will know you asked great questions by the respondent's body language.

Enjoy the Silence

Many of us are uncomfortable with silence. We feel the need to fill the space with words. However, whenever you feel the urge to speak, remember the time you said to yourself after a conversation, "I wish I would have said _____." You don't want to leave a conversation with the other person thinking that. Give them space to formulate their answers. Further, some of the most experienced moderators who ask questions for a living will say someone's first answer isn't usually their final (or best) answer. The gems come after they have had time to think about it.

State It Simply

Sources on how to ask better questions will often challenge you to ask your question in five words or fewer. This is hard to do and can be a lofty goal but is key to asking clear and unbiased questions. We find it common to initiate questions with statements. *Back when I was your age, I didn't have a cell phone. We used phone booths and wrote letters. How do you think your relationships are different than mine were as a twenty-something?* This entire dialogue could be simplified to: *How do you think relationships in your generation compare to older generations?* Statements, or backstory to questions, offer little value and run the risk of bias or directing people toward a certain answer. This is also called a *leading question*. While "five words or fewer" is a challenge, work on simplifying your questions to as few words as possible.

Why, What If, and How?

Warren Berger is an expert at asking questions. He has several books and a website, amorebeautifulquestion.com, with several tips and a question index. One guidance he offers when asking questions to spark ideas (and we would argue insights) is the three-question trinity: Why? What if? And how?

In his books and talks, he applies these three questions to the invention of the Polaroid camera. *Why* do we have to wait for the picture to develop? *What if* the picture could be developed inside the camera? *How* can we make that happen? In insight discovery, *why* and *what if* are excellent tools to help dive deeper into a perplexity. Why is the perplexity happening? What if we could address this? How can we make that happen? The *how* is what we would call "activation of the insight."

Hindsight/Insight/Foresight

The why, what-if, and how framework is one we are particularly fond of because it sets up the opportunity to be future-oriented in our application of insights. It also aligns with another framing of how we interpret data: hindsight/insight/foresight.

Hindsight is analyzing our past. It interprets data with a framing of "if I knew then what I know now . . ." Hindsight also assumes the best predictor of future behavior is past behavior. There is truth in this statement. Humans are inherently risk averse and prefer the status quo. We rely on lessons from our past experiences, which is why we end each chapter with a case. Hindsight is limiting, however. It does not set us up for innovation or disruption.

Insight is our present state. As we have already defined, it is a deeper understanding of our behavior. It answers our intuitive next question after we uncover a pattern, pain point, perspective, or perplexity—why? Having the skill to uncover an insight is the first hurdle—and the purpose of this book. The second hurdle is to activate it (our next book?).

Foresight is what we envision the future state to be based on our insight. If we don't have a good insight, then we are limited in our ability to see what is possible. With Trapper Keeper (from Chapter 4), there was a pattern revealing that kids are disorganized and want to be cool; foresight is seeing how a new binder would keep papers in place and make a school supply desirable. In Chapter 5, Cialis uncovered the pain point of time pressure—four hours to be exact—for a couple to be intimate. The team explored the question, "What if couples could regain their spontaneity?" The Luvs case in Chapter 6 described how the marketing team went deeper than uncovering how second-time moms feel but how they wanted to feel—what if we could validate second-time moms, that they are good moms because they have experience? Each of these three examples from our prior chapters demonstrates how great brands went beyond the pattern, pain point, or perspective (insight) to a future state (foresight).

This brings us to the case of perplexities, which will be different from the last three chapters. In this case, we will *not* focus on a brand or company but rather on data that supports a perplexity between physicians and patients and a research study that evaluated the "what if." This case will further support the premise that insight discovery and activation are not limited to the marketing of brands but can also have applications in a broader context, such as the areas of medicine and public health.

CASE: *"THE BIRTH CONTROL FOR ME IS NOT FOR YOU"*

"The What"

When patients are given a medical choice, they often ask their doctors, "What would you do?" It seems logical enough that physician preference would offer credibility and direction. They have more experience, education, and information than the average patient. Seeking a healthcare professional endorsement is not new. Trident chewing gum made the "Four out of five dentists agree . . ." a popular cliché. The assumption is physicians would recommend based on their beliefs and preferences.

You could argue contraception is about as common as gum chewing for adult women. According to the CDC, 98 percent of all women twenty-five to forty-four have used contraception. Further, for this same age group, 82 percent have used three or more different contraception methods. Logically, you would conclude women healthcare providers and their patients would have similar preferences when it comes to birth control.

This conclusion would be false. A study published in 2014 compared birth control selection among healthcare professionals that work in women's health clinics with the general population. The results: women healthcare providers make vastly different personal contraception choices than their patients. This finding was picked up by mainstream media in articles such as:

- "This Is the Birth Control Most Doctors Use" *(Women's Health Magazine)*
- "When Doctors Pick Their Own Birth Control, IUDs are the Most Popular Options" (Vox website)

As the article titles suggest, healthcare professionals most often use an IUD (intrauterine device) as contraception, while patients most often use sterilization (a procedure often referred to as a "tubal" or having your "tubes tied" to permanently prevent pregnancy). Why is an IUD so popular among healthcare professionals? Here are a few quick facts:

- An IUD is inserted into the uterus and can be effective anywhere from three to twelve years, depending on the specific device selected

- IUDs work by either emitting the hormone progestin or copper, which creates a uterus that prevents sperm from reaching an egg. Copper is a natural repellant for sperm, and hormones will create a thick mucus in the cervix, which blocks sperm from moving to the egg for fertilization. Hormones can also prevent ovulation—no ovulation, no egg to fertilize, no pregnancy
- IUDs are effective. According to the CDC, IUD's failure rate is less than 1 percent. By comparison, birth control pills are 9 percent and condoms are 17 percent
- Hormonal IUDs have the added "benefit" of reducing the amount of blood and/or duration of the user's menstrual cycle

How different are professionals from patients? The graph below compares the results from the survey with healthcare providers working in a family planning function with a survey representing the general population of women ages twenty-five to forty-four.

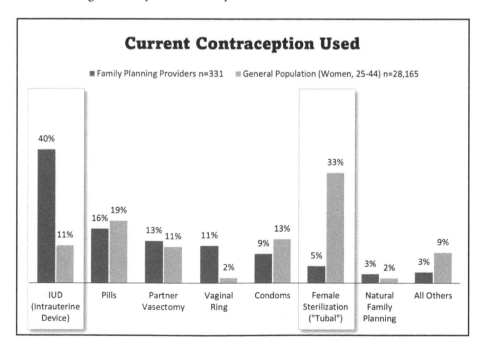

Current Contraception Used

■ Family Planning Providers n=331   ■ General Population (Women, 25-44) n=28,165

- IUD (Intrauterine Device): 40% / 11%
- Pills: 16% / 19%
- Partner Vasectomy: 13% / 11%
- Vaginal Ring: 11% / 2%
- Condoms: 9% / 13%
- Female Sterilization ("Tubal"): 5% / 33%
- Natural Family Planning: 3% / 2%
- All Others: 3% / 9%

Two specific perplexities stand out. Women healthcare providers select an intrauterine device (IUD) almost four times more often than the general population. Next, patients select female sterilization (often referred to as having your tubes tied) six-and-a-half times more often than healthcare providers. Media picked up on the perplexity associated with IUDs, but what about sterilization? Is there more that this data is telling us? What do these two methods have in common? Both are effective, long-term options and do not require anything after the procedure. A conclusion from this data is that many women desire a contraception option that is both effective, long-term, and easy.

"The Why"

To investigate this perplexity, the next inquiry to explore are barriers to women choosing an IUD. For this, we found a published literature review that summarized both physician and patient barriers to IUD use. It should be noted the review was focused on barriers among women who had not yet had a pregnancy, so we are assuming this can be extrapolated to all women seeking birth control. Three main patient barriers were reported. These are:

1. **Awareness.** The exact number of women aware of IUDs as an option varies depending on the study; however, the range reported was 55–60 percent unaware (or 40–45 percent aware).
2. **Fear and concerns.** The most common concerns among women regarding an IUD are the risk of an ectopic pregnancy, fear the insertion procedure will be too painful, and concern over a change in their menstrual bleeding pattern.
3. **Cost.** While there is evidence to suggest the cost would be lower than other options when extrapolated to the duration of use, the initial cost can be prohibitive. Out-of-pocket costs for the device, plus the cost for the office visit, can reach more than $1,000 in

the United States, with no reimbursement from an insurance or government provider.

From a barrier perspective, there are some intuitive similarities between selecting an IUD and having a sterilization procedure. First, both require a procedure. Any procedure is associated with risks as well as an added level of scheduling and planning. Lastly, both can also have cost implications. A sterilization procedure can reach upwards of $5,000–$6,000.

"The What If"

What if we could remove the barriers of awareness, fear/concern, and cost? If these barriers could be addressed, how many women would choose an IUD as their form of birth control? The Contraceptive CHOICE Project did just that. In 2006, an anonymous foundation provided funding for a study at Washington University in St. Louis. This study enrolled more than 9,000 women in the St. Louis area who were fourteen to forty-five years old and desired to avoid pregnancy for at least twelve months. All participants were sexually active or planned to be and were open to trying any reversible contraception method—sterilization was not included as an option in this study.

All the women who enrolled received counseling to review all possible contraceptive methods. This included effectiveness, advantages, and disadvantages. Models of all methods were available. Further, a demonstration of the IUD insertion procedure was provided. The participant was then allowed to choose the contraception they preferred at no cost for up to three years (assuming no contraindications). They were allowed to change their minds anytime and as many times as they desired during the study period with no cost implication. These steps essentially removed the three main barriers: awareness, education to address concerns, and fears about the cost.

The results? IUDs were the most commonly selected contraception among the women in the study at 58 percent (combining the copper and hormonal options). While there are other interesting outcomes of this study, for our purposes, removing the most common barriers means achieving a level similar to healthcare professionals for IUD use.

"The How"

Unfortunately, continuing to receive anonymous donations to continue the CHOICE project is not a feasible solution to remove barriers to the selection of an IUD for birth control. Based on the CDC, the current use of IUDs is similar to the original study referenced at the beginning of the case—within ten years it has increased about 2 percent. Perhaps this speaks to the enormity of the barriers to be removed. We are not experts in public health, medical education, reimbursement, or any of the groups that would drive "the how" in this case . . . beyond awareness. *As marketers, we are pretty good in that area.*

We hope this case leaves you a bit unsettled. Our other cases are wrapped up with a nice success story of how the insights were pulled through to execution. Unfortunately, we find this to be more of a rarity than the norm. We have seen plenty of insights be discovered only to get shelved because we could not answer the question, "So now what do we do?" Typically, to activate an insight, you must apply two mindsets: 1) Think in a future state (what if), and 2) engage a diverse set of skills and expertise. This second part is a challenge since we often don't work well cross-functionally.

We hope this case leaves you with two key takeaways:

1. You view perplexities as a positive; they identify something new to explore deeper
2. Insight discovery and activation is a team sport. Not only do we benefit from learning about others' perspectives (Chapter 6), but we also need diverse experiences and skill sets to act on our insights

Practice: Perplexity Exploration

The next time you identify two data points that seem valid but lead to different conclusions, use it as an opportunity to evaluate further.

1. Dive deeper into the sources from both data points. Who? How many? What instruction?
2. Write one new conclusion based on your review of the sources. Do you have a potential explanation or theory about how both data points could be "right"?
3. Draft one new question based on the source exploration that could further foster your insight discovery.

SECTION 3:

CONNECTING THE DOTS—BUILDING INSIGHT CAPABILITY AND COMPETENCY

We buy things we don't need with money we don't have
to impress people we don't like.
—Dave Ramsey, American personal finance personality
and radio show host

"Dave Ramsey & Dave's Double"—Road-Tripping with Mitch and Melinda

In our consulting together, we had a period of five years when we drove from Indianapolis to Chicago to work with clients about every six weeks. The drive is three-and-a-half hours one way—too short to fly but long enough to run out of things to say. Typically, our drive to Chicago was lively as we prepared for our meetings, shared our stories from the prior weekend, and planned our dinner. The return home was a different story. It was often at night after a full day of meetings, and we were brain-dead. Even for Mitch, who doesn't like silence, talking was exhausting.

At some point in our travels, we discovered a mutual interest in the Dave Ramsey podcast. This became our drive home routine—in addition to stopping at the same Wendy's/gas station for our celebratory "Dave's double" and fries.

If you are unfamiliar with Dave Ramsey, he is an American personal finance personality and businessman. His company produces an educational series, books, and syndicated radio shows/podcasts centered on simple steps to get out of debt and build wealth. That might sound like a boring way to spend three-plus hours in a car late at night, but Dave has a special style that speaks to his broad audience. He is kind and encouraging to those that follow his principles. He has many folksy sayings that make you chuckle. The most entertaining, however, is his blunt style. Dave has no problem calling something stupid.

The callers into the *Dave Ramsey Show* come from all financial backgrounds and situations. And even though the questions become repetitive when you have listened to as many episodes as we have, the behavior of continued listening speaks to an insight: Money is personal, and people do not want to admit it when they are at fault for their financial decisions. Further, just like with a diet or an exercise program, discipline and awareness of our activity comprise the first step to taking control. To quote Dave, "A budget is telling your money where to go instead of wondering where it went."

No matter the situation, Dave stays on message. He has a clear "seven baby steps" system proven to help people get out of debt and get control of their finances. Wherever the caller is, he points them to the right "baby step" for direction. Even though callers are often overwhelmed by their situation, Dave's approach is fairly consistent. He listens, then asks questions. If the listener is open and engaged, Dave presents a simple solution to get them on the right baby step and commits to supporting them (such as sending the caller one of his books). Callers that debate or challenge Dave's wisdom is another (entertaining) story.

In Dave's podcast, he applies his approach at an individual/couple/family level that is supported by books and tools. Dave also developed his Financial Peace University and offers regular live seminars, which create the opportunity to imbed the financial independence mindset at a community level. We want to take a similar approach with this final section of the book.

Consider Section 2 on pillars the bachelor's level degree on insights. This section is the master's level part of the book. The pillars will only get you so far. To take insight discovery to the next level, there are two components: at an individual or group level and the broader organization.

In Chapter 8, we will describe the process of synthesis for your specific insight discovery. Synthesis will help you strengthen your insight by connecting the dots between all of your sources and pillars. Chapter 9 will provide evidence of the value of an organization being insight-driven as a strategic competitive advantage. This chapter will include the key characteristics an insight-based company should embrace because they have been proven to lead to greater revenue growth than their competition.

CHAPTER 8:
SYNTHESIS—STRENGTHENING YOUR INSIGHT FOUNDATION

According to the map, we've only gone four inches.
—Jeff Daniels as Harry Dunne in Dumb and Dumber (1994)

"You're Putting Too Much Food in Your Mouth"—Melinda

I wasn't an athletic kid growing up. I was active enough but never good at a team or individual sport. In my early twenties, I made fun of "those people" that do things like run or count their macros. Then I had my first kid, a son, and turned thirty. Many things hit me at those milestones: 1) I wanted to be healthier so I could be active with my son, and 2) I knew I could no longer eat whatever I wanted and still fit into my pre-pregnancy clothes. This was also the time when I was about to start my business.

My overall goal for starting the business was to achieve a better work/life balance. In the process of starting the business and thinking about my goals, I commented to my husband, "I wonder if I could complete a half-marathon." You should know my husband is an avid runner, completing a half marathon or two in a year. In the fall of that year, he signed me up for the next race. At this point, I could not run a mile without stopping. Signing me up forced my hand. Could I take this on? After a friend encouraged me to run it with her and helped me train, I am proud to say, not only did I finish the race, but I also became one of those people I sneered at—a runner.

Running proved to have several benefits for me. First, I got in great shape. I was in better shape than before my pregnancy—probably even better than in my early twenties. I found I could still eat all my favorite foods. When I overindulged one day, I just ran more the next. I also found it became a stress reliever. No matter what happened in the day, if I went for a run, I knew I had accomplished something that day many people could not accomplish during their lifetimes.

Fast-forward several years, and we have our daughter. While I was pregnant with her, I was diagnosed with borderline hypothyroidism. This required blood work at every visit for the rest of the pregnancy. I learned during this process that a synthetic hormone is available if my symptoms and levels did not improve.

A year after delivering a beautiful and healthy baby girl, I was still carrying ten extra pounds despite running my fourth half-marathon. Knowing hypothyroidism can impact weight, I asked my OB/GYN to test my levels, assuming this was the obvious problem at my yearly appointment. Her response was, "I don't think that's it. I think you are putting too much food in your mouth." I'm sure the look on my face said enough. She agreed to order the blood test but then asked me to agree to start a food diary when the results came back normal.

To my dismay, everything was normal. After a week of being honest about what I was eating in my food diary, the answer was obvious . . . and my doctor was right. I could no longer outrun my poor food decisions. The ten pounds wasn't going to come off with a synthetic hormone. My diet would require the level of discipline I had put into my running schedule.

We picked this story to start the chapter because, for Melinda, running was like a "pillar-based" insight. She uncovered the benefits of running and assumed they would become her solution. Running makes her feel young and invincible. Her doctor was seeing multiple data points and synthesizing them into a different solution. We do something similar in insight discovery. We get excited when we uncover something using a pillar as a tool, but it is one-dimensional. It is the entry level for insight discovery. This chapter will outline a process called *synthesis* to pull learning from each of the 4 Pillars into a better and more comprehensive view of your customer. One pillar alone can start the germination of an insight, but the strength is in the combined understanding of multiple pillars.

Teams we work with are often overwhelmed by the amount of data they have, the enormity of their problem, and the fear of making the wrong decision. They hold a belief the perfect answer is out there. They are also held to timelines and a desire to work at a faster pace. Synthesis is the next level of thinking. It is harder than focusing on one or two of the pillars because it will take time and discipline, will be met with the internal barriers we just mentioned, and requires practice.

Synthesis vs. Summary

Summarizing is a skill we are encouraged to perfect throughout our education. Whether it is writing a paper or taking notes in a class, summarizing is distilling information into manageable chunks to represent the key points or findings from a source. *Synthesis* is the next step and what we call the "work" of arriving at an insight. With synthesis, you are making connections between those key points in your summary (including what you learn from your 4 Pillars) to create new findings and (hopefully) an insight or further refining of an insight.

To state it simply, synthesis is hard. Making connections between data and information sources to arrive at a new idea or insight is rarely done alone. Our individual bias and general mental capacity to manage multiple data sources can be overwhelming. While an individual can start the synthesis process, it should be a collaborative and inclusive activity. One of the greatest challenges we see at organizations is the delegation and expectation of synthesis to reside in teams with analytical responsibilities and/or with a market research agency. This is often a result of the volume of data available to be processed and an irrational fear of statistics. While these groups will play an important role in synthesis, and therefore insight discovery, they can lack the "big picture" mindset to see connections. Synthesis requires the ability to do a deep dive on a dataset and then pull up to a high-level view to explore the "so what." While there are a few individuals who can do both, they are hard to find and still have their own biases.

A few key points to remember about synthesis:

- Synthesis is making connections between sources to arrive at new information and/or an insight
- While any of the 4 Pillars can facilitate the development of an insight, synthesis will help refine and deepen your understanding of that insight
- The results from the 4 Pillars and synthesis will be better when working with a team that represents cognitive diversity

Getting to the Deep Truth

A theme is simply a connection that exists between data sources or a conclusion from a data source. Themes can become an insight on their own, help teams answer business problems, and/or aid in solution creation. As you examine all the data you have available, you will likely apply all or most of the 4 Pillars to construct themes. As you apply the learning from your pillars, you will continue to make connections, ultimately arriving at that deep truth—the insight.

A common framework used in insight discovery is the "data-to-insight pyramid." There are many versions, but essentially, data is the base; then there is a layer above that (sometimes called knowledge, interpretation, findings, conclusions, etc.); then at the top is insight or wisdom. Here is the visual we propose exists for insight discovery:

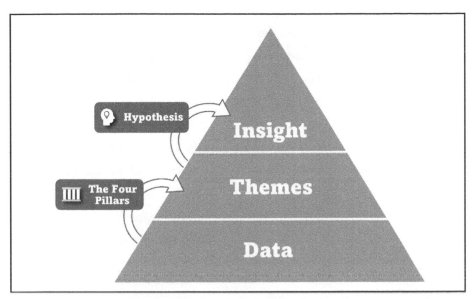

In each of the 4 Pillar chapters, we identified a theme using data to represent chronic obstructive pulmonary disease (COPD) sufferers and/or treaters. Here is a recap of what we provided in each chapter.

- In Chapter 4: Patterns—we provided physician and patient quotes (qualitative research) and a published study (quantitative research) to support the pattern theme that *physicians are not communicating a COPD diagnosis to their patients*
- In Chapter 5: Pain Points—a visual depiction of a patient journey for COPD was given. At the top of the journey was the overall conclusion: *The patient is on a long and slow route, failing to recognize symptoms and smoking history, while the physician takes a shortcut to the COPD diagnosis.* The pain point is a patient's failure to recognize their symptoms and connect them to their smoking history to realize they might have COPD. Once the patient is diagnosed, we called out a moment of truth for the patient, "shock and shame"
- In Chapter 6: Perspectives—we took the patient journey in Chapter 5 to a deeper level to uncover how the COPD patient wants to feel. Specifically, we surmised *COPD patients want to be seen and*

their condition validated by being included among the scientific community as an area of focus and innovation

- In Chapter 7: Perplexities—despite two different numbers from sources, we concluded ***COPD underdiagnosis is a problem*** in the market. Further, we uncovered a tension between patients and physicians: ***The patient's smoking history could represent shame and blame, which prevents specific conversations about their condition***

In Chapters 4 through 7, we got a deeper understanding of COPD as a condition. Now let's bring those into an insight hypothesis. In Chapter 3, we introduced you to the hypothesis framework we recommend.

- Because: What evidence is supporting your hypothesis?
- Belief: Start your statement with, "We believe . . ." to describe a hypothesis. What do you believe is the "deep truth" or insight?
- Behavior: What will you do if your hypothesis is proven to be true?

This framework helps connect your learning from the 4 Pillars to arrive at a deeper meaning. Taking our COPD themes, here is an example of a hypothesized insight.

Because:	• Physicians are not formally communicating the COPD diagnosis to their patients (Chapter 4)
	• Patients do not connect their smoking history to their symptoms whereas physicians apply the smoking history to predict and anticipate a COPD diagnosis (Chapter 5)
	• Patients feel shame and blame about their smoking history which prevents specific conversations about their condition with their physician (Chapter 7)
	• Patients want to be seen and validated that their condition is an area of focus in the medical community (Chapter 6)
We believe:	COPD is a "secret diagnosis"
Therefore, we will (behavior):	Develop a campaign to help patients see themselves included in a widespread condition that is supported by a broader community (i.e., a ribbon or bracelet type campaign)

When we work with a cross-functional group, they will often have more than one hypothesis and will come up with something better than the research team. For example, "secret diagnosis" (shown in the visual) came from a participant group at one of our live learning sessions. We had been teaching this case for eight years—no one had used that phrase before, yet it is the best description we have heard of the insight to date. Ideally, we like to see two to five different working hypotheses, if possible. If there is only one hypothesis, there is little room for deeper debate and discussion, while more than five can create too much debate and hinder activation.

Short Cuts to Insight Discovery: Behavioral Economics

Getting to the hypothesized insight is hard, even though it seems simple enough. The idea might be percolating but difficult to describe. We recommend teams visit behavioral economic (BE) principles to spark ideas. BE is a relatively new field of research that blends psychology, economics, and the scientific method to examine the human rationality of decision-making. Research has shown that humans (even the most educated) often behave irrationally, changing their actions when the same choices are framed differently. We see this when a superior option is available and yet is not chosen frequently, when attitudes don't match behavior, or when stated intentions don't translate into action.

BE principles have been compiled by economists to help make sense of and predict irrational behavior. Each principle describes at a high level how the majority of people will behave under specific circumstances. Some of the most common BE principles we see in insight discovery are below.

Default

People tend to choose the easiest option or the path of least resistance to avoid complex decisions. Defaults provide a mental or cognitive shortcut and signal what people are supposed to do.

Examples:

- Fast-food restaurants will often default to a size for your meal combo. You may be prompted with, "Is large, okay?" Regardless, you, as the customer, have to opt out of the pre-determined size and request a different size when ordering
- Physicians prescribe a particular brand of medication not because it has been proven better, but because it happens to be the default option in the hospital's electronic ordering system

Loss Aversion

People strongly want to avoid losing and therefore tend to stick to existing or standard behavior rather than doing something different. Studies show, in general, losses are more painful than gains are pleasurable.

Examples:

- Most contestants on the *Jeopardy* game show always start at the top of the board where the questions are easier, and the losses are smaller if they miss a question. This is loss aversion at work. But remember James Holzhauer? James, who earned a living as a gambler, used a different strategy. He played the bottom of the board first, choosing the higher-dollar questions and then moving up the board. By answering the higher-dollar amounts first, he took more money off the table, therefore making it harder for players to catch him
- Researchers have shown how loss aversion can help to incentivize employees. They did a study where they divided workers into three groups. The first was a control group, which was not given a bonus. The second group was promised a bonus at the end of the year, based on meeting specific goals. Participants in the third group were given a bonus at the beginning of the year and were told they

would have to pay it back if they did not meet specific goals. The workers in the first two groups performed about the same, but those in the third group performed significantly better

Social Proof

People want to be like everyone else and are heavily influenced by what they perceive everyone else is doing.

Example:

- For those of us who have donated blood, you are typically given a sticker to wear upon leaving the blood center that says, "I donated blood today." That little sticker given to you takes the un-witnessable activity of you giving blood and makes it a witnessable activity to everyone who you will encounter for the rest of the day. The blood center hopes others will see the sticker and give blood because you have done it and made it visible to others
- Many of us are conditioned to only purchase items online with an average rating of 4.5 out of 5 stars and a minimum of 1,000 reviews. This offers the proof we need that one product is better than another and worth the purchase

In practice, these principles can't be changed but can help to understand connections in our themes. Bringing it back to our COPD example, social proof is one way to activate a desired behavior, encouraging a conversation between patients and physicians about COPD to foster proper treatment. The BE principle can help teams with either the belief or behavior statement in their hypothesis.

There are many other BE principles to be considered than what is shown here. We highly recommend the Center for Advanced Hindsight associated with Duke University for information on various principles, research, and relevant articles.

Now What?

At this point in your insight discovery journey, you have a hypothesis—or a few. You should feel accomplished; most teams we work with struggle to get to this step. Your work, however, is not done. Here are the next key steps to take your hypothesis into implementation.

1. *Validate outstanding assumptions and concerns*

You should anticipate some challenges and questions that remain after you share your insight hypothesis. As we have stated throughout this book, insight discovery is about conversation and debate. Activating your insight will require the same level of engagement from stakeholders in your organization. Invite them to share their thoughts. Everyone processes information and concepts at a different pace. Be sure to share a simplified version of your process to uncover the insight with what is needed by the stakeholder: data, quotes, published validation from a trusted source, etc. We also like to recommend a question: "What would you need to see to prove this is true or not?" Recognize that these proof points might not be possible, but they help uncover the rationale for any objections.

These conversations around your hypothesized insight will generate outstanding questions (IWIKs—I wish I knews). Be sure to exhaust these questions and concerns but set the expectation that not all questions can or will be answered.

The next step is to prioritize these questions and then revisit the insights. This will be an iterative process. As you gather new information, expect your hypothesis to evolve, and if you have more than one hypothesis, you must consolidate the information to a smaller list. Our guidance for marketing teams activating an insight is to align to *one* core market insight based on your prioritized stakeholder group.

2. *Incorporate insights into brand development*

With increased competition and access to customers using new formats, brand development has increased in importance for a wide range of industries, including with artists and influencers. Those new to brand development will often focus on the tangible elements: colors, logo, font, and tagline, for instance. While these elements are important, they should be the expression of a more critical component—positioning.

Simply stated, *positioning* is the space you want your brand to occupy in the mind of the customer. Who is the brand for? What does the brand stand for? How is the brand unique? Why should your customers care? These are all the foundational questions for your brand's positioning in the market. Your core marketing insight should be the source of truth to answer these questions.

Let's take a non-traditional branding example. Think about what it is like to be a fan of any artist, sports team, or group. Being a fan says something about you. It connects you as a member of a group with a common interest. The Grateful Dead fans are Deadheads; Green Bay Packers fans are Cheeseheads; fans of the TV show *Veronica Mars* are called Marshmallows. Being a fan and associating yourself with a name is connected to a deeper humanistic insight. *We associate ourselves with a group to fulfill our need for belonging. We want to feel connected to someone or something greater than ourselves.*

An artist that understands this better than anyone is Taylor Swift. If you are a Swifty, you will of course like the music, but what else connects you to her? Besides being an artist and musician, what words would you use to describe Taylor Swift? Kind? Approachable? Caring? Genuine? Taylor Swift has cultivated a connection with her fan base that is praised and envied by other artists. Of course, she has the tangible elements of her brand: the music, the color red, etc. Yet her brand is deeper than what you see and hear. She has facilitated a feeling, not just among other fans, but with her directly. She is a standout in the collection of beautiful blonde singers.

3. *Pull through your insights in your communication*

When planning your brand communication, you will probably work with an external agency for the creative elements. The creative brief is the document to ensure this tangible communication is addressing your objective and is aligned with the tangible and intangible elements of your brand. We are fans of the book *The Creative Brief Blueprint,* written by Kevin McTigue and Derek Rucker. Most teams we work with do not write their own creative briefs—or if they do, they are overly simplistic and do not give clear direction. As McTigue and Rucker describe it, "A proper creative brief provides all the necessary information to guide the team to produce the desired outcome so that you get the output you want." You will not be surprised to see *insight* as one of the six core components they outline in their book. Insight helps your creative agencies "offer a provocative way to demonstrate the insight and the benefit."

4. *Continue to evolve the insight*

The early part of insight discovery is both frustrating and exhilarating. Getting to a single core insight to be foundational to all your marketing activity is a marathon. As a result, you may feel the desire to be done altogether or protect the insight from any doubters or challengers. Both reactions can lead you to stop learning about the insight. This is dangerous. Our customers are complex and so too is the insight we have about them. Keep a passion for learning all you can about your customer, and this will keep your insight alive and strong. Here are some areas where you can continue to grow and evolve your understanding of a customer and their insight.

- Language: Words matter. To quote Jonah Berger from his latest book *Magic Words,* "Words do more than just convey information." Some words have deeper connections and meaning than others for different people. Do you have a full understanding of the words your customers use? Do you know what words have more meaning than others?

- Context and Influence: Data, messages, and touchpoints are all around us. What does your customer engage with regularly? What sources do they value more than others?
- Desired State: Never underestimate the power of representing how your customer wants to feel. Even if you already know your fans want to feel connected and a part of a group, continue to ask, "Why?"

Your Turn

We did not end this chapter with a specific case. Rather, we offer an opportunity for you to practice your insight discovery. In Appendix I, we have a collection of data from a variety of sources about retirement. Specifically, we want to explore the question, *Why don't people save more for retirement?*

Using the problem statement format, we introduced in Chapter 3 of Section 1, here is how we would suggest defining this problem:

Problem Statement

Retirement is defined as the time of life when one chooses to permanently leave the workforce behind for good and stop working. Planning for retirement is a personal journey. The amount one needs to save depends on one's age, income, desired retirement income, inflation, and more. For many Americans, savings rates—especially for retirement savings—are woefully low. In 2019, the average retirement account savings for American households was $65,000. The majority of Americans report they are behind in their savings, with only 20 percent reporting to be right on track with their retirement savings. According to the latest annual Transamerica Center for Retirement Studies survey, almost three in four workers (73 percent) agree with the statement, "I am concerned that when I am ready to retire, Social Security will not be there for me." So why are people not saving more for retirement?

The Assignment

Part 1: The 4 Pillars

Turn to Appendix I to review a collection of data points already summarized from a variety of sources. After reviewing this data, apply the 4 Pillars, using the following as a guide:

Patterns	• What are the repeated ideas within and across these sources?
Pain Points	• Along the journey to retirement, what are the critical moments that represent tensions, frustrations, realities, or unmet needs with regard to saving?
Perspectives	• How do people feel about saving for retirement—and how do they want to feel?
Perplexities	• Where are there disconnects in the data sources?

As you work through the sources and 4 Pillars, keep notes of your outstanding questions. Once you exhaust the sources we provided, what questions could you easily answer with additional research and information? Gather this information and revise your conclusions and findings for each pillar.

Part 2: Hypothesis Generation

Using the framework provided in this chapter, what is your hypothesis for why people do not save for retirement? What is potentially that one core humanistic insight that prevents us from saving more for retirement? Again, your hypothesis should have the following three elements:

- Because: What evidence is supporting your hypothesis?
- Belief: Start your statement with, "We believe . . ." to describe a hypothesis. What do you believe is the "deep truth" or insight?
- Behavior: What will you do if your hypothesis is proven to be true?

Part 3: Validation

We do not provide an answer to this case for several reasons.

- Insight discovery requires discussion and debate—there is no one right answer
- The insight will evolve as our data and understanding of retirement changes
- We plan to use the case in future classes as a teaching example

Despite these reasons, we do not want to leave you empty-handed. We invite you to have a conversation with us about this case. Email us at submit@findinginsightbook.com and provide your answers to the pillar questions and your hypotheses. We will offer feedback, ideas, and future questions. **Those of you who rise to the occasion of tackling the case and make significant attempts at the Pillars and hypotheses will get something in return—an endorsement from us in the form of an email, letter, and/or LinkedIn digital endorsement.**

CHAPTER 9:
BECOMING AN INSIGHTS-BASED ORGANIZATION

Nobody really knows what they're doing.
Some are just better at pretending like they do.
—Kumail Nanjiani, Pakistani-American comedian

"Blue Dots and Blue Roofs"—The First Mitch and Melinda Road Trip

We kicked off this section talking about our many road trips to Chicago, but our first road trip was actually to Nashville, Tennessee. We started working together when a small biotech company was looking for a situation analysis in the obesity space. Specifically, what was the landscape for approaches to address obesity in the United States and what were the opportunities and barriers to a pharmaceutical agent in the market? While we had never worked together during our shared time at Lilly, we had a colleague in common that connected us based on our skill sets.

The obesity market is one ripe for an insight discovery and one of the reasons we use it as a teaching case in our learning programs. To conduct a proper situational analysis, we believe it requires both a market research and marketing perspective, which align with our skills and strengths. Our first step in the process was to review all secondary data sources to gather key facts and data points—this was Melinda's role. Some of what she uncovered included:

- Americans consider obesity to be as serious a health problem as cancer
- Among obese adults, 43 percent correctly classify themselves as obese (vs. normal weight or overweight)
- Nearly all Americans with obesity have tried to lose weight at some point
- Physicians believe patients lack the discipline to lose weight

Most surprising was the fact that less than 1 percent of obese adults were taking a prescription drug for weight loss despite there being several medications available on the market. This was before the new medications on the market today, like Wegovy and Zepbound. In fact, before these newer agents, many pharma companies had given up on pursuing a prescription solution for obesity and weight loss due to all the hurdles involved in achieving success and their failed attempts—this was Mitch's role. He identified all the barriers to entering into the category, and there were many.

After discussing all our findings and conclusions, we hypothesized an insight: "Obesity is seen as a 'people problem' and not a pill solution."

The dilemma for us was how to tell our client that the low percentage of patients receiving a prescription medication was actually a market opportunity if they leveraged our insight. The opportunity for success, as we saw it, was to be non-traditional. Don't offer a pill solution alone. Our face-to-face presentation had us a bit nervous, to say the least. A traditional pharma company would probably stop listening after learning how few patients were on drug therapy. How would this company respond to this non-traditional recommendation?

We started with the facts about the market. The team, which included the CEO and his direct reports, seemed interested, intrigued, and engaged. Whew! Off to a good start. Next, Mitch shared the six hurdles we believed the company would need to overcome if they were to be successful. Still, the team was open and engaged in a positive discussion. They were not deterred by the challenge. But they gave us a new challenge. An upcoming board meeting had been scheduled to make a go or no-go investment decision for pursuing an obesity indication for one of their pipeline assets. We were instructed to go away and prepare a presentation for the upcoming board meeting, which included our insight and recommendation to be more than a pill solution.

On our way back from our first meeting with the client, we discussed the challenge of how to tell a story to best communicate to the board the opportunity and the risks in making their final decision. The good news was the CEO was open to a non-traditional approach to the market. They didn't ask us to leave when we revealed what we believed to be the core insight. They did the opposite. The team embraced the idea they were not "big pharma" and could think differently. This was exciting for us, if not a bit daunting.

As we crossed over the state line from Tennessee into Kentucky, there was major construction on the interstate, and we were forced to take a detour onto the back roads of the Bluegrass State. We noticed some of the houses had blue roofs consistent with Pantone 286, which is the official color of the Kentucky Wildcats sports teams. Talk about a dedicated fan base. This triggered an idea for how we would go about telling our obesity landscape story to the board.

When presenting to executives, the temptation is to show a bunch of slides with dense charts and tables. A better and more engaging way is to communicate a story with a simple picture we sometimes call the "money slide," which is one used to tell the whole story. We decided to convey the overall size of the obesity market using a grid of gray dots with each dot representing a million people with obesity. Orange dots were used to convey within the gray dot grid how many patients were on a branded prescription product using traditional pharma promotional efforts. A traditional pharma company would fight it out among those few orange dots, maybe grow the market by a dot or more. Using the insight that obesity is seen as a "people problem" and not a pill solution, we recommended a non-traditional approach strategy using blue dots to denote the opportunity for a pill to complement a customized weight-loss program using some innovative non-pharma partnerships and tactics. Our message: Don't fight it out with the orange dots; convert the gray dots to blue dots. Blue dots represent what we learned to be true—people are engaged in multiple weight-loss strategies. Incorporate the prescription with these strategies rather than replace them.

This was an easy and effective way to convey the situation, the insight, and the strategy, all in one picture. It was well received by the board and many commented that it was so simple, they could easily convey this story to potential investors for what became known later as the "blue dot" strategy. As you can imagine, this was not only rewarding for us but a learning moment. The senior leadership team and the board comprised a good mix of business experiences and cognitive diversity in their thinking. Not only were they open-minded, but they were also excited to hear something not traditional. The idea of doing something different in the space was energizing, as they wanted to experiment and were not afraid of the potential risks.

Unfortunately, the product did not move forward with clinical development, but for us, so much more came out of this project. We deepened our approach to situation analysis. We developed a teaching case for our future insight discovery learning programs. And we kicked off what has been one of the longest and most rewarding personal and professional partnerships for two people who could not be more different.

More than a Class

We could not complete this book without coming back to the earlier questions Mitch posed in his *Why This Book* section as it relates to a company becoming an insight-based organization. But what does it mean to become an insight-based, or what some would call a "customer-centric," organization?

It's estimated there are more than 43 billion devices connected to the internet worldwide. Being customer-centric is imperative in a connected world because traditional business drivers don't cut it anymore. Anyone can produce quality products, and manufacturing no longer provides a sustainable competitive advantage. These capabilities are table stakes today, according to Driest, Sthanunathan, and Weed in their 2016 HBR article "Building an Insights Engine." They write that the new source of competitive advantage is customer centricity: deeply understanding your customers' needs and fulfilling them better than anyone else. The ability to transform data into insights and turn those insights into strategy is what increasingly separates the winners from the losers.

In a recent conversation with a senior business executive of a Fortune 500 healthcare company, summed it up best, "There is something about going 'all in' with customer insights as the foundation for all business decision-making and creating a competitive advantage in the market. Get this correct and then you are on your way to a successful business. Get this wrong, and you leave yourself vulnerable to competitors taking your business." We could not agree more with this statement about going "all in" with customer insights as the foundation for creating a competitive advantage. Often, we are contacted by clients who have bought into the value of insights but believe a training program is all they need. To truly build an organizational capability as described in the HBR article, it takes more than a class.

The Essentials Ingredients for Building an Organizational Capability

It begins with thinking about the bigger picture and the foundational elements needed to build this type of mindset and capability across an entire organization. We believe the essential ingredients for building and sustaining any organizational capability are:

- **Process:** includes well-defined workflow processes and collaborative ways of working including metrics, standards, etc.
- **Tools:** leverage the latest technology platforms, easy-to-use frameworks, process maps, etc.
- **People:** utilize a collaborative organizational structure with the right talent, training, and personnel management to improve and reward knowledge, skills, behaviors, and performance
- **Culture:** shared beliefs, values, and written and unwritten rules that have been developed over time and guide member behavior

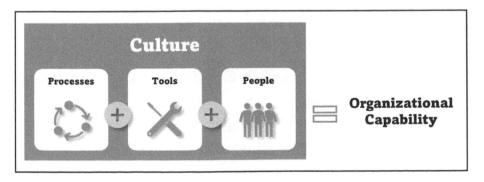

We would propose culture is foundational to success in building any organizational capability. We have personally experienced helping organizations build a process for insight discovery, along with thinking frameworks, tools, and training modules, only to see them fail because the culture and leadership were not "all in." They were not fully obsessed (in both actions and words) with a singular focus on understanding and meeting customer needs first. They were reluctant to equip the broader organization with the resources, structure, and support needed. Nor were they willing to embrace the risk and experimentation needed to become an insight-based organization.

As we consider the essential ingredients for building this type of "all in" capability for insights, we go back to another one of Mitch's earlier questions: *What can we learn from business academia and successful organizations when it comes to building an insight-based capability?*

Learning from Others

At the beginning of 2015, the Insights2020 (i2020) global market research study began and was led by Millward Brown Vermeer in partnership with The Advertising Research Foundation (ARF), ESOMAR (European Society for Opinion and Market Research), LinkedIn, Kantar, and Korn Ferry. The global initiative was built on the findings of Marketing2020 and was the largest global marketing and insights leadership initiative of its kind, focused on aligning insights and analytics strategy, structure, and capability to drive business growth. This research focused on:

- The role of insights and analytics in driving business strategy and growth
- Organizing the insights and analytics function—structure and processes
- Building the capability—equipping the function for success
- Emulating leadership competencies of over-performers

Between March and September 2015, more than 325 interviews and 10,000 surveys were conducted with business, marketing, and insights/analytic leaders worldwide in more than sixty countries. Companies were divided based on three-year revenue growth relative to their competitors into the following two groups:

- **Over-performers** (outpaced competitors in revenue growth)
- **Under-performers** (those that lagged behind)

Frank van den Driest, former partner at Kantar Consulting and Founder of The Institute for Real Growth, was one of the keynote speakers at ESOMAR when the first wave of results was presented from the i2020 study. Driest pointed out that in this age of the connected customer, four things stand out related to companies being able to achieve real growth through customer-centricity. They are:

1. Ability to activate insights across the entire customer journey
2. Access to whole, new, rich, and relevant data sources, like behavioral data sources
3. Ability to personalize product and service offerings better than ever before
4. Ability to link everything they do to their brand purpose

In addition, he stated there are significant internal organizational challenges in many companies that need to be overcome to achieve real growth. These mainly revolve around operating in silos, bureaucracy, and the legacy of a function or structure. These challenges characterize more of the under-performers. Whereas, the over-performers were more concerned about making sense of the data rather than which function or structure was responsible. It's not that silos don't exist in the over-performing companies. The over-performers just do a better job of creating a layer of collaboration culture across those silos.

Out of sixty-six variables tested in the quantitative part of the study, ten variables clearly stood out that characterized the over-performers versus the under-performers (see table below).

Building an Insights Engine

	Over-performers	Under-performers	Difference
Data synthesis *Ability to link different data sources to distill insights – one version of the truth*	67%	34%	**33%**
Affinity for action *Active participation in strategic decision making*	79%	47%	**32%**
Whole-brain mindset *Combing analytical and creative thinking*	71%	42%	**29%**
Experimentation *Embrace a culture of experimentation*	40%	13%	**27%**
Business focus *Demonstrate business acumen*	75%	50%	**25%**
Storytelling *Communicate with engaging narratives*	61%	37%	**24%**
Collaboration *Work closely with other functions, suppliers, and consumers*	69%	52%	**17%**
Independence *Head of insights reports directly into c-suite*	29%	12%	**17%**
Integrated planning *Insights involved in all key stages of the planning cycle*	61%	46%	**15%**
Forward-looking orientation *Substantial future orientation*	32%	28%	**4%**

The one that stood out most to us and represented the greatest difference between over-performing and under-performing companies was data synthesis (a 33 percent difference). This is one of the major reasons we wrote this book—because many companies and organizations lack a defined process for linking different data sources to get to an insight. None of the companies studied complained about a lack of data. The enormous increase in data availability was given the term "infobesity." Often, the challenge is working across different and disparate data sets. These data sets are usually owned by different teams or, in some cases, different companies. To leverage the power of the data they possess, over-performers centralize ownership into "one source of truth" and organize into "expert communities" that collaborate to turn data into actionable insights.

Other key variables that showed double-digit differences between over-performers and under-performers were affinity for action (32 percent difference), whole-brain mindset (29 percent difference), business focus (25 percent difference), storytelling (24 percent difference), and collaboration (17 percent difference).

Let's look at one of the largest consumer goods companies, Unilever, and how they transformed themselves by focusing on these key variables to build a superior insights engine for revenue growth.

CASE: *"BUILDING THE UNILEVER INSIGHTS ENGINE"*

As mentioned earlier, the *Harvard Business Review* featured the paper, "Building an Insights Engine—How Unilever Got to Know Its Customers," which focused on the findings from the Insights2020 Research and how the insights engine has been applied to Unilever's culture, structure, and capability development. For those not familiar with Unilever, it is a large consumer goods company with 400-plus brands, including Dove, Hellman's, and Ben and Jerry's (to name just a few), with sales of over $60 billion in 2022. In the article, the authors describe their insights engine and how it works to underpin their corporate customer-centric strategy.

The Unilever executives explain how they embodied the ten characteristics of a superior insights engine taken from the i2020 research study within and across the organization. The characteristics are divided into two broad groups: operational characteristics and people characteristics. Here are just a few examples of how they have gone about building their insights capability:

Operational (Processes and Tools)

- **Data Synthesis:** Implemented a global marketing information system, accessible to all marketers throughout the company that ensures all users have "one version of the truth." The authors note in the article that this has dramatically reduced the debates about data definitions, methodology, and interpretation, which has led to competing (and sometimes wrong) conclusions

- **Independence of Insights Function**: Superior insight groups sit decisively outside marketing and other functions and often report to someone in the C-suite. At Unilever, the executive vice president for consumer and market insights now reports to a member of the executive board who leads marketing, communications, and other business functions

- **Integrated Planning**: The insight's function participates throughout the entire planning cycle from strategy (defining "where to play") through tracking and advising on tactical adjustments that may improve performance

- **Collaboration**: Every employee is encouraged to engage with customers about their needs and provides tools to help. Anyone within Unilever can mine its 70,000 documents and vast social media data to gain insights about consumer needs. To record their insights, employees use an in-house app that captures observations from live chats or other consumer interactions

- **Experimentation**: Started a "Shark Tank" initiative borrowed from the ABC show with the same name for internal teams to pitch new technologies to the executive team. Each has five minutes to tell its story followed by five minutes of Q&A. After the presentations, the executive team votes on which ideas to pilot and which ones to reject

People

- **Staffing**: Invests in development programs designed to expand people's competencies beyond the expected functional skills (research and analysis) to "action" skills—communicating, persuasion, facilitation, and leading

- **Storytelling**: Unilever has moved away from presenting charts and tables and more toward provocative storytelling with memorable TED-style talks embracing an environment of "Show. Don't Tell"

As you can see from the Unilever example, building an insight capability requires more than a training class and is broader than just an analytics function. The incorporation of defined processes, a collaborative structure, an array of tools, the right people who possess the necessary skills for discovery and activation, and most importantly, a culture and leadership obsessed with meeting the needs of their customers is essential for success. This means taking the voice of the customer into account in every business decision, which also means it must be embraced by all functions in the company. It requires a culture of collaboration and leadership from the top to ensure every function—from R&D to marketing to insights and analytics—maintains a singular focus on understanding and meeting customers' fundamental needs.

For answers to additional questions posed by Mitch in his "Why This Book" section, see Appendix II.

FINAL THOUGHTS

Our original conclusions for this book were fairly simple. First, we wanted to deepen your understanding of an insight. If you find yourself more selective in your use of the word insight, then perhaps we have met this goal. Second, we wanted to bring practical tools into the insight discovery process. Often, we see insight discovery being limited to a specific skill set or function. Throughout all our years working in marketing and marketing research, we know this is too short-sighted. If we have truly deepened your understanding of an insight, then you know statistical analysis and customer market research are tools but not the only tools for insight discovery.

As we solidified our content, examples, and cases, we kept coming back to the same three themes and found these to be the true conclusions for uncovering the non-obvious obvious.

1. **Get comfortable being uncomfortable.** The greatest barriers for insight discovery all have one thing in common: they tend to make us uncomfortable. Whether it is uncovering your bias, embracing debate and diverse thinking, seeking out others much different from you, or being open to being wrong, the more uncomfortable you are, the more likely you are learning something new. The more likely you are about to uncover an insight.

2. **Insight discovery is a team sport, but it needs a facilitator.** We cannot emphasize enough the role of cognitive diversity and cross-functional involvement in insight discovery. However, someone needs to lead and facilitate the work. This might mean someone tasked with organizing the data following one of the pillars, facilitating a hypothesis brainstorming session, or even proposing the hypothesized insight to a team for discussion. Inviting others to participate in the process will improve your skills equal to the practice of the skills we outlined in this book. If you practice with the retirement facts and submit your thoughts to us, be sure to first invite others to challenge your thinking.

3. **New questions can be more valuable than new insights.** Another key component of the insight discovery process is uncovering new questions. Hopefully, we have impressed upon you that insights do not happen on a timeline; the discovery is not a linear process, and you are never truly done learning about why people do what they do. Be curious and never stop asking *why.*

To close, as Gary Klein observed in his book, *Seeing What Others Don't,* "Although we may not be able to predict the exact instant when a person has an insight, the process is not as mysterious as many people think." We hope the simple tools, frameworks, and skills we have conveyed in this book have removed some of the mystique in uncovering what we all want to know: a deep truth that explains why people do what they do.

ACKNOWLEDGMENTS

Cognitive diversity is a strong theme in our book. We fundamentally believe critical thinking and the resulting work product is better with more and diverse minds on the task. For this reason, we have several groups that we felt strongly needed to be acknowledged even though it is impossible to name them all.

Our Work Family

If you look at the total hours in your day/week, you likely spend more time with your co-workers and colleagues than your family. We are blessed to have a collection of people we work with who have become extended family members. Starting with Cathy Allen, for whom we could not work or live without. Cathy's dedication to the people she surrounds herself with is a rare and cherished trait. She truly puts others before herself. We will never know the full extent of the time and sacrifices she has made for us. Every compliment from her is sincere and every challenge or critique comes from the right place. Ashley Hawkins, who created all of the visuals in this book, is equally creative and kind. She embraces any challenge we throw her way and then asks if there are more ways she can help. Kim Hoffman has given us a foundation of support through the many evolutions of our companies. She has been our cheerleader and our third-party conscious. Everyone should have a Cathy, Ashley, and Kim in their corner.

There are members of our extended work team who are not involved in our day-to-day or have moved on to other endeavors that continue to influence our thinking represented in this book. Elizabeth Ridenour, Tom Nash, John Hixon, Lisa Fleming, and Paul Bishop—thank you! We hope you read this book and see elements of things we have worked on together and a recognition of the part you played.

Extra special recognition goes to our good friend and mentor, Rich Pilnik, who was the catalyst for our initial and ongoing business collaboration.

Our Personal Family

Writing a book takes time. Even though other authors told us this, we still underestimated the time and involvement. As a result, our personal family had direct and indirect involvement (whether they realized it or not). Melinda's husband, Jeff, has been her devoted partner since pairing up in chemistry class and more recently our partner in Practical Marketing Skills. Gavin, Rylan, Sandi, Doug, and Rob thank you for your contributions to the personal stories. Kathleen (Melinda's mother), you were our first full reader of the book, and your engagement meant more than you know—I just wish Dad was alive to read it as well. Mitch's wife, Julie, probably invested the most time and editorial talent from both our families. Without her support and encouragement, this book would have never moved much beyond the introduction.

Fellow Authors and the Morgan James Team

We are fortunate to have a few authors in our network who offered guidance, advice, and connections. Kim Saxton, Tim Calkins, Kevin McTigue, and Alex Perry, we would not have a published book without you. We also would not have a published book without the Morgan James team. To David Hancock, thank you for the opportunity, confidence, and faith you placed in us in writing our first book. Jim Howard, for helping us finalize perhaps the most important part of book—the title. And to Addy Normann for helping us navigate the production process. The experience, mentoring, and support exceeded our expectations, and we are humbled to be one of your authors. And last but not least, Cortney Donelson, your patience and attention to detail is second to none and you made sure the words on the pages throughout remained true to our voices.

Content Contributors and Reviewers

Much of the content in this book came from our own work and life experiences, from participants who have attended our learning programs over the past ten years, and from those authors and teachers that we look up to as "giants" in critical thinking. However, we would be remiss if we did not mention those specifically who helped shape and inform the content. Special thanks to Jay Justice who allowed us to use his personal story as an example at the beginning of the Perspectives chapter. Also, special recognition to Tony Ezell for reviewing early parts of our initial manuscript to provide ideas, suggestions, and direction.

Mentors, Colleagues, and Clients

Last but not least we have a collection of mentors, former colleagues, and clients. We are all a product of our experiences and there are so many of you that have shaped and influenced us. We hope all of you read this and make a personal connection to a piece of content in the book.

APPENDIX I:
RETIREMENT DATA AND FACTS

Source #1: "Recognizing and Addressing Risks and Realities Negatively Impacting Retirement Security"; New report explores demographic influences on US workers' long-term financial outlook. Press Release from TransAmerica Center for Retirement Studies, November 30, 2021.

- 24% of US workers are very confident that they will be able to fully retire with a comfortable lifestyle.
- Retirement confidence varies by demographic segment. Outlined below: % very confident about their future retirement.

By household income:

- Less than $50,000: 11%
- $50,000–$99,999: 14%
- $100,000+: 34%

By location:

- Urban: 32%
- Suburban: 19%
- Rural: 16%

Employment status:

- Full-time: 25%
- Part-time: 15%

- Quotes from Catherine Collinson, CEO and President of Transamerica Institute and TCRS:
  - *Demographic influences can profoundly affect a worker's ability to save, plan, and prepare for a financially secure retirement. A greater understanding of these influences can help identify opportunities, envision solutions, and inform public policy priorities for strengthening our retirement system.*
  - *Strengthening our retirement system is best accomplished through collaborative efforts among policymakers, industry academics, nonprofits, employers, and individuals. Every stakeholder plays an important role. By increasing our understanding of demographic influences, we can more effectively address inequalities and implement solutions that serve all.*
- 82% of workers are saving for retirement through their current employer's 401k or similar plan and/or outside of work.
  - *Workers with a household income of $100,000+: 91%, vs. income of less than $50,000: 60%.*
- 34% of workers have taken a loan, early withdrawal, and/or hardship withdrawal from 401k, IRA, or similar plan.
- Workers have saved $93,000 in all household retirement accounts (estimated median).

Estimated median of household retirement accounts by household income:

- Less than $50,000: $3,000
- $50,000–$99,999: $47,000

- $100,000+: $200,000

- 49% of workers indicate debt interferes with their ability to save for retirement.
- 33% of workers have a written financial strategy for retirement.
- 73% of workers are concerned that social security will not be there for them when they are ready to retire.
- 80% of full-time workers are offered a retirement plan vs. 51% of part-time workers.

Source #2: "Four Generations of Workers Are Preparing for Retirement Amid an Uncertain Future"; New research examines the retirement prospects of Baby Boomers, Generation X, Millennials, and Generation Z. Press Release from TransAmerica Center for Retirement Studies, October 12, 2022.

Baby Boomer Workers (Born 1946 to 1964):

- 40% expect social security to be their primary source of retirement income.
- 83% are saving for retirement in an employer-sponsored 401k or similar plan and/or outside the workplace.
- Median age to begin saving: 35.
- Those participating in a plan contribute 10% (median) of their annual pay.
- Estimated median saved: $162,000 in total household retirement accounts.
- Estimated median saved in emergency savings: $15,000.
- 49% expect to or are already working past age 70 or do not plan to retire. Their reasons:
  o *Healthy aging-related: 78%.*
  o *Financial-related: 82%.*

Generation X Workers (Born 1965 to 1980):

- 22% are very confident they will be able to fully retire with a comfortable lifestyle.
- 28% strongly agree they are building a large enough retirement nest egg.
- 78% are concerned social security will not be there for them when they are ready to retire.
- 81% are saving for retirement in an employer-sponsored 401k or similar plan and/or outside the workplace.
- Median age to begin saving: 30.
- Those participating in a plan contribute 10% (median) of their annual pay.
- Estimated median saved: $87,000 in total household retirement accounts.
- Estimated median saved in emergency savings: $5,000.
- 38% expect to retire at age 70 or older.
- 55% plan to work in retirement.
- 27% have a financial strategy for retirement in a written plan.

Millennial Workers (Born 1981 to 1996):

- 34% were unemployed at some point during the pandemic.
- 60% cite paying off debt as a financial priority.
- 73% are concerned social security will not be there for them when they are ready to retire.
- 76% are saving for retirement in an employer-sponsored 401k or similar plan and/or outside the workplace.
- Median age to begin saving: 25.
- Those participating in a plan contribute 15% (median) of their annual pay.

- Estimated median saved: $50,000 in total household retirement accounts.
- Estimated median saved in emergency savings: $3,000.

Generation Z Workers (Born 1997 to 2012):

- 52% experienced one or more negative impacts on their employment ranging from layoffs, furloughs, reduction in hours and pay.
- 51% have trouble making ends meet.
- 67% are saving for retirement in an employer-sponsored 401k or similar plan and/or outside the workplace.
- Median age to begin saving: 19.
- Those participating in a plan contribute 20% (median) of their annual pay.
- Estimated median saved: $33,000 in total household retirement accounts.
- Estimated median saved in emergency savings: $2,000.

Source #3: "Generational Views of Retirement in the United States." National Institute on Retirement Security. July 2021.

	Baby Boomers	Generation X	Millennials
% Agree: America is facing a retirement crisis.	72%	69%	64%
% Agree: The average worker cannot save enough on their own to guarantee a secure retirement.	70%	65%	68%
% Concerned: How concerned are you that you won't be able to achieve a financially secure retirement?	43%	59%	72%
% Likely: How likely is it that you will need to work past the normal retirement age to have enough money in retirement?	52%	52%	78%

Source #4: "Economic Well-Being of U.S. Households in 2022"; Board of Governors of the Federal Reserve System. May 2023.

- 27% of adults in 2022 considered themselves retired.
- Sources of retirement income for all retirees are:
  - *Social Security: 78%.*
  - *Pension: 56%.*
  - *Interest, dividends, or rental income: 42%.*
  - *Wages, salaries, or self-employment: 32%.*
  - *Cash transfers other than Social Security: 9%.*
- Forms of retirement savings among non-retirees:
  - *Defined contribution pension: 54%.*
  - *Savings not in retirement accounts: 47%.*
  - *IRA: 34%.*
  - *Defined benefit pension: 20%.*
  - *Other retirement savings: 11%.*
  - *Business or real estate: 8%.*
  - *None: 28%.*
- % Non-retirees indicating their retirement savings is on track by year:
  - *2017: 38%.*
  - *2018: 36%.*
  - *2019: 37%.*
  - *2020: 36%.*
  - *2021: 40%.*
  - *2022: 31%.*

	% Any Retirement Savings	% Retirement Savings on Track
Age group:		
18–29	57%	24%
30–44	72%	32%
45–59	81%	34%
60+	88%	41%

Race/Ethnicity		
White	80%	37%
Black	60%	22%
Hispanic	56%	20%
Asian	84%	38%
Disability Status		
No disability	76%	34%
Disability	47%	13%
Overall	72%	31%

- Among non-retirees, % mostly or very comfortable investing self-directed retirement savings:
  o *Men, high school degree or less: 36%.*
  o *Men, some college/technical or associate degree: 41%.*
  o *Men, bachelor's degree or more: 60%.*
  o *Women, high school degree or less: 22%.*
  o *Women, some college/technical or associate degree: 27%.*
  o *Women, bachelor's degree or more: 32%.*
- Assessment of financial literacy questions:

Question on . . .	% Answered Correctly	% Didn't Know	% Answered Incorrectly
Interest	69%	19%	12%
Inflation	67%	24%	9%
Diversification	45%	51%	4%

- Note: Survey of Household Economics and Decision-Making was fielded October 21–November 1 2022. Survey was fielded by a private consumer research firm using an online panel. 11,667 participated and completed the survey.

Source #5: "Economic Well-Being of U.S. Households in 2021"; Board of Governors of the Federal Reserve System. May 2022.

- 27% of adults in 2021 considered themselves retired.
- Sources of retirement income for all retirees are:

- o *Social Security: 78%.*
- o *Pension: 57%.*
- o *Interest, dividends, or rental income: 43%.*
- o *Wages, salaries, or self-employment: 32%.*
- o *Cash transfers other than Social Security: 11%.*
- Forms of retirement savings among non-retirees:
  - o *Defined contribution pension: 55%.*
  - o *Savings not in retirement accounts: 52%.*
  - o *IRA: 36%.*
  - o *Defined benefit pension: 22%.*
  - o *Other retirement savings: 13%.*
  - o *Business or real estate: 10%.*
  - o *None: 25%.*

	% Any Retirement Savings	% Retirement Savings on Track
Age group		
18–29	62%	30%
30–44	75%	39%
45–59	84%	45%
60+	87%	52%
Race/Ethnicity		
White	81%	46%
Black	64%	26%
Hispanic	61%	25%
Asian	85%	52%
Disability Status		
No disability	79%	43%
Disability	49%	17%
Overall	75%	40%

- 8% of non-retirees borrowed or cashed out their retirement savings in 2021.
- Among non-retirees with less than $50,000 in retirement savings, 12% had borrowed from or cashed out retirement savings accounts

in the prior 12 months. This is 7% among those who had $50,000 or more.

- Among non-retirees, % mostly or very comfortable investing self-directed retirement savings:
  - *Men, high school degree or less: 37%.*
  - *Men, some college/technical or associate degree: 45%,*
  - *Men, bachelor's degree or more: 64%.*
  - *Women, high school degree or less: 29%.*
  - *Women, some college/technical or associate degree: 26%.*
  - *Women, bachelor's degree or more: 33%.*
- Assessment of financial literacy questions:

Question on . . .	% Answered Correctly	% Didn't Know	% Answered Incorrectly
Interest	69%	19%	12%
Inflation	64%	26%	10%
Diversification	43%	53%	4%

- Indicating they are at least doing okay financially:
  - *Among those who answered all three financial literacy questions correctly: 89%.*
  - *Among those who answered 2 of the 3 financial literacy questions correctly: 79%.*
  - *Among those who answered 1 of the 3 financial literacy questions correctly: 69%.*
  - *Among those who answered 0 of the 3 financial literacy questions correctly: 64%.*
- Note: Survey of Household Economics and Decision making was fielded October 29–November 22, 2021. Survey was fielded by a private consumer research firm using an online panel. 11,874 participated and completed the survey.

Source #6: "Defined Contribution participation, savings rates keep ticking up amid uncertainty—Vanguard," Margarida Correia, June 7, 2022.

- In 2021, 81% of employees eligible to participate in their employers' retirement savings plans did so. In 2016, this rate was 71%.
- Plans with auto-enrollment had a participation rate of 93%, while those that did not had a participation rate of 66%.
- In 2021, 42% increased their contributions, 7% decreased, 2% stopped, and 49% left their contribution rate unchanged.
- Median contribution rate was 10.4% (author suggests this should be 12–15%).
- Note: The Vanguard Report is based on 1,700 qualified plans, 1,400 clients, and ~5 million participant accounts for which Vanguard provides record-keeping services.

Source #7: Bankrate survey, September 21-23, 2022.

- % of Americans say their retirement savings are:
  - *35% significantly behind.*
  - *20% somewhat behind.*
  - *20% right on track.*
  - *8% slightly ahead.*
  - *7% significantly ahead.*
  - *10% didn't know where they stand.*

Generational Group	% Indicating Ahead (significantly + slightly)	% Indicating Behind (significantly + slightly)
Generation Z	31%	30%
Millennials	19%	46%
Generation X	9%	65%
Baby Boomers	7%	71%

Income Group	% Indicating Ahead (significantly + slightly)	% Indicating Behind (significantly + slightly)
Less than $80,000 per year	13%	59%
$80,000-$99,999 per year	17%	54%
$100,000+ per year	23%	46%

- American's reported contribution to retirement accounts this year compared to last year:
  - *8% significantly more.*
  - *17% slightly more.*
  - *34% about the same.*
  - *7% slightly less.*
  - *9% much less.*
  - *24% not contributing this year or last year.*
- Among those contributing the same, slightly less, or much less, selected reasons for not contributing more to retirement this year (multiple selections allowed):
  - *54% inflation.*
  - *24% stagnant or reduced income.*
  - *24 % new expenses.*
  - *23% debt repayment.*
  - *22% desire to keep more cash on hand.*
  - *18% market volatility.*
  - *7% don't want or need to increase contributions.*
  - *7% don't know.*
  - *5% something else.*

Generational Group	% Increased Contributions	% Decreased Contributions
Generation Z	30%	10%
Millennials	30%	18%
Generation X	19%	17%
Baby Boomers	22%	18%

Education Group	% Increased Contributions	% Decreased Contributions
High School Diploma or less	20%	15%
Some College	21%	21%
4-year College Degree	33%	13%
Post-Graduate Degree	36%	14%

- Note: Survey was conducted for Bankrate by phone interview from September 21–23, 2022. Sample size: 2,312 American adults.

Source #8: Financial literacy, longevity literacy, and retirement readiness. The 2022 TIAA Institute-GFLEC Personal Finance Index.

- The 2022 P-Fin Index survey was designed to be indicative of retirement readiness, financial literacy test, and gauged longevity literacy.
- The P-Fin Index financial literacy test shows the following relationships between answering questions correctly and . . .
  - o *Saved for retirement on a regular basis.*
  - o *Tried to figure out how much needed to save for retirement.*
  - o *Knowledge about ways to draw income from savings during retirement.*
  - o *Ease (vs. difficulty) to making ends meet in a typical month.*
  - o *Spend less time per week thinking about and dealing with issues and problems related to personal finance.*
  - o *Are more satisfied with their current financial situation.*
  - . . . among current retirees.
- The P-Fin Index financial literacy test results among workers age 40 and older based on a sample of 1,219 workers.

		% of P-Fin Index Questions Answered Correctly			
	All	25% or less	26–50%	51–75%	76–100%
Saving for retirement on a regular basis	72%	54%	59%	78%	90%
Saving for retirement is unconstrained by debt payments	67%	61%	58%	68%	78%
Have tried to determine how much is needed to save for retirement	47%	25%	38%	51%	68%
Confident about saving an adequate amount for retirement (among savers)	73%	73%	68%	71%	81%

- Longevity literacy was measured based on those who correctly answered the following:

  o *Life expectancy: [if male] for a 60-year-old man in the US (answer: about 22 more years or age 82) or [if female] for a 60-year-old man in the US (answer: about 25 more years or age 85).*

	Answered Correctly	Don't Know	Overestimate	Underestimate
US Adults	37%	28%	10%	25%
Men	32%	27%	11%	31%
Women	43%	28%	10%	19%
Generation Z	30%	36%	7%	27%
Generation Y	32%	32%	9%	28%
Generation X	37%	26%	8%	29%
Boomers	44%	23%	13%	20%

% of P-Fin Index questions answered correctly	Answered Correctly	Don't Know	Overestimate	Underestimate
25% or less	20%	52%	7%	20%
26%–50%	34%	33%	10%	23%
51%–75%	44%	16%	12%	28%
76%–100%	52%	10%	12%	27%

Among workers age 40 & older	Knowledge of the Life Expectancy for a 60-year old			
	Strong Knowledge	Poor Knowledge	Overestimate	Underestimate
Saving for retirement on a regular basis	80%	53%	80%	73%
Saving for retirement is unconstrained by debt repayments	73%	63%	67%	59%
Have tried to determine how much is needed to save for retirement	56%	28%	51%	48%
Confident about saving an adequate amount for retirement (among savers)	78%	69%	73%	69%

Source #9: Financial Literacy Around the World: Insights from the Standard & Poor's Ratings Services Global Financial Literacy Survey.

- According to a recent survey conducted by Standard & Poor's, only 57% of US adults are financially literate.

  Note: The Government Accountability Office defines financial literacy as "the ability to make informed judgments and to take effective actions regarding the current and future use and management of money. It includes the ability to understand financial choices, plan for the future, spend wisely, and manage the challenges associated with life events such as a job loss, saving for retirement, or paying for a child's education."

APPFNDIX II:
ADDITIONAL QUESTIONS ANSWERED

B elow are some of the commonly asked questions Mitch posed in his upfront section of the book that we are continually asked when working with organizations. Caution: The answers provided are based on our beliefs, personal biases, and 55+ years of experience. We recognize that some of you as readers may have different views or perspectives.

How do we equip marketers to recognize an insight from a fact, observation, or opinion?

As mentioned earlier in Chapter 2, insight discovery can be learned, taught, and mastered. Most people have never had any formal training or education when it comes to uncovering an insight and rely solely on their market research or creative agencies to do the work. However, it should not be expected that people will attend one or two training classes and automatically have the process mastered. Training alone will not automatically make people proficient and/or insight experts. To be proficient requires practice, practice, and more practice, along with time and experience to become an investigator and aggregator of insights. In addition, we stress in our insight learning programs that the goal is not to make everyone an insight expert. It is to understand how the process works so one can ask the right questions when working with their insights/analytics functions and/or creative agencies to become a better consumer of insight research.

What skills and competencies are required to excel at uncovering and activating insights?

Throughout Section 2 of this book, we have included in Chapters 4–7 guidance as it relates to the critical skills and competencies, we believe are necessary to excel at uncovering insights. In summary, we believe the following skills are critical: the ability to write a good problem definition, the ability to summarize patterns of data while avoiding conclusions, the ability to explore and observe others' behavior while suspending judgment, the ability to actively listen to learn while avoiding selectively hearing to confirm, the ability to ask a great question to get to a deeper understanding, and the ability to synthesize data by linking different sources to arrive at one version of the truth.

Should a brand focus on a single insight or many at a time?

With so much data available ("infobesity") today, teams struggle to get to a single core insight their brand can own and leverage, especially if the market or category is crowded. As shown earlier in the cases of Luvs and Cialis, both brands uncovered a single core human insight they could successfully activate and leverage in all facets of their promotion for many years. From our experience, more is not better. We see teams struggle when trying to execute more than one insight at a time. This leads to a loss of focus and, more importantly, confuses customers. We believe, if possible, a brand should focus on the activation of a single core insight.

What barriers will we need to overcome, both at an individual and company level, to become more of an insights-based organization?

We dedicated Chapter 2 of this book to why insights are so hard to find both at an individual and company level. Some of the barriers we addressed in the chapter are ones we have personally witnessed or experienced in our careers. Personal bias, stereotyping, being judgmental instead of curious, ignoring habits, and others were mentioned and described as personal barriers. On an organizational level, we addressed groupthink, organizations placing their own priorities over the needs of customers, and in Chapter 9, the siloed organizational mentality.

Once we have an insight, how do we pull it through from strategy to execution so it does not get lost?

We often see teams find a good insight only to see it become lost when it comes to the strategy and execution of a brand. This can happen for various reasons. Some team members don't believe this is the insight yet and want to keep investigating. In addition, marketers tend to fall in love with their brand's physical and functional features and don't know how to fully activate the emotional component to their advantage. Some have already decided what the strategy is, and if the insight doesn't support it, then it is ignored. The creative agency has its own idea of how the brand should be communicated and experienced, which results in campaign ideas that don't completely bring the insight to light. So how does one ensure the insight is pulled all the way through to execution?

As mentioned in Chapter 7, we believe the entirety of insight discovery and activation is a team sport. It requires debate and aligning on the actual insight. Once the core insight is agreed upon by all team members, it should then be central to the strategy and execution. Since execution is usually carried out by various agencies (e.g., creative, digital, consumer, etc.), we recommend marketers write their own master creative brief (not the agency), clearly communicating the insight to be activated. When the agencies bring forward their creative ideas, the master brief becomes the standard by which those ideas are evaluated for selection and execution. This process requires a certain discipline by all parties involved for successful pull-through from analysis to strategy to execution.

Who on a team decides whether the insight is a good one?

As mentioned previously, insight discovery is a team sport. However, we do see key roles within a marketing team that shepherd an insight from identification to activation. If it is assumed that the market research function will be the ultimate owner and champion of insights, you will not have an insight-based organization. Rather you need a senior member who believes in the insight and the relationship of the insight to brand performance. Here are the suggested roles we see on a team:

- **Insight Investigator and Facilitator**: This is typically a market research/analytics function that collects, organizes, and (hopefully) synthesizes data to facilitate a team discussion on insights. They may support insight hypotheses, but we would argue they are not the ultimate decision-makers on the final insight

- **Insight Champion**: This should be the most senior marketer on the team with accountability for brand performance. Their role is to champion the insight throughout the team and organization. You could argue that this person will have the final say on whether the insight is a good one or not, given their role

- **Insight Activators**: Anyone working on brand planning, strategy, or execution is playing a role in activating the insight. While they may not be the ultimate decision-makers, they are stewards for the success of activating the insight

ABOUT THE AUTHORS

Mitch Tull is the founder and principal of Marketing Skill Partners LLC, a global consultancy that advises marketing capability leaders from leading pharmaceutical and health-  care companies on the marketing foundations required to deliver top-line business results. An experienced pharma- ceutical executive with expertise in global and healthcare marketing, Mitch held numerous marketing leadership positions during his thirty-plus years with Eli Lilly and Company, including leading Lilly's Marketing Institute. Mitch is also the co-founder of Practical Marketing Skills, LLC, a special- ized marketing content provider that exists to strengthen critical thinking skills where market research and brand marketing intersect with each other. He received a Bachelor of Science degree in Pharmacy from the University of Arkansas and lives in Carmel, Indiana with his wife, Julie.

Melinda Spaulding is the co-owner and president of Prac- tical Insights, Inc., a marketing research consulting firm, and co-founder of Practical Marketing Skills, LCC, a spe-  cialized marketing content provider. Market research has been central to Melinda's career, beginning with her Masters in Market Research from the University of Georgia. She was Eli Lilly & Company's first hire from this program as a market research consultant. Melinda shifted to the service side of market research, which included running the analytics function and serving on the executive committee for G & S Research. In 2007, she and her husband established Practical Insights, Inc., allowing her to grow beyond primary market research projects. Today, Melinda is sought after for her ability to synthesize data, connect insights to strategy, and share the art of storytelling. She currently lives in Cicero, Indiana.

ENDNOTES

SECTION 1 REFERENCE SOURCES

"Hindsight, Insight and Foresight: Key Ingredients for Effective Planning," Meeting Magic, accessed August 16, 2023, https://meetingmagic.co.uk/blog/hindsight-insight-foresight-key-ingredients-effective-planning/.

Chapter 1: What Is an Insight?

Dalton, Jonathan. "What Is Insight? The 5 Principles of Insight Definition." Thrive. January 6, 2023. https://thrivethinking.com/blog/.

"Stan Sthuanunathan, Unilever: Building a World-Class Insights Engine." Center for Customer Insights at Yale. January 1, 2017. Video, 37:31:00, https://www.youtube.com/watch?v=T8-h2zBgRp0.

Davidson, J. E., & Sternberg, R. J. (1984). "The Role of Insight in Intellectual Giftedness." *Gifted Child Quarterly*, 28(2), 58–64.

"Haha and aha! Creativity, idea generation, improvisational humor, and product design," Barry M. Kudrowitz, DSpace@mit.edu, 2010.

Ma, Moses. "The Power of Humor in Ideation and Creativity." *Psychology Today*, June 17, 2014.

Ward, A. and A. Cole. "Comedy and Strategy: Don't Laugh, This is Serious . . . Ok Laugh." Art of War Blog, November 14, 2016.

Subramaniam, Karuna. "The Behavioral and Neural Basis for the facilitation of Insight Problem-Solving by a Positive Mood," Arch: Northwestern University Institutional Repository, December 5, 2008, last modified October 2, 2018.

Merchant, Brian. "The Secret History of the iPhone." The Verge. June 2017, accessed August 22, 2023, https://www.theverge.com/.

"15 years of the iPhone: When the cellphone became a personal computer," Market Research Telecast, January 2022.

Eadicicco, Lisa. "This Is Why the iPhone Upended the Tech Industry," *Time Magazine,* June 29, 2017, accessed August 20, 2023, https://time.com/4837176/iphone-10th-anniversary/.

Pink, Daniel H. 2017. *A Whole New Mind: Why Right-Brainers Will Rule the Future.* 2nd ed. New York: Riverhead Books.

Brunski, Jeff. "Chapter 14, Concept Generation Part Deux." Product Development Distillery, July 19, 2019, https://medium.com/product-development-distillery/chapter-14-concept-generation-part-deux-95ad21a95a86.

Chapter 2: Why Are Insights So Hard to Find?

Becker, Howard S., 1998. *Tricks of the Trade; How to think about your research while you're doing it.* Chicago. University of Chicago Press, Ltd., London.

Mion, Landon. "Southern accents could cost job seekers a 20% wage penalty, study finds," *New York Post,* May 27, 2023.

Wedell-Wedellsborg, Thomas. 2020. *What's Your Problem? To Solve Your Toughest Problems, Change the Problems You Solve.* Boston: Harvard Business Review Press.

Duhigg, Charles. 2012. *The Power of Habit: Why We Do What We Do in Life and Business.* New York: Random House Publishing Group.

Martin, Neale. 2008. *Habits: The 95% of Behavior Marketers Ignore.* Upper Saddle River, New Jersey: FT Press.

Klein, Gary. "Seeing What Others Don't: The Remarkable Ways We Gain Insights." PublicAffairs, 2013, https://www.amazon.com/Seeing-What-Others-Dont-Remarkable/dp/1610392515/ref=tmm_hrd_swatch_0?_encoding=UTF8&qid=&sr=.

Travis, Daryl & Yates, Harrison. 2014. *How Does It Make You Feel? Why Emotion Wins the Battle of Brands.* Brandtrust. Networlding Publishing.

"Curiosity Is an Innovation | Cassini Nazir | TedXUNT." YouTube. December 2, 2021. Video, 7:13:00, https://www.youtube.com/watch?v=DZ8bIcleplE.

Grant, Adam. 2021. *Think Again: The Power of Knowing What You Don't Know,* New York: Random House Publishing Group.

Davidson, Janet E. and Robert J. Sternberg. "The Role of Insight in Intellectual Giftedness." *Gifted Child Qurterly*, Volume 28, Number 2, Spring 1984.

Klein, Christopher. "Why Coca-Cola's 'New Coke' Flopped." (history.com), April 23, 2015, https://www.history.com/news/why-coca-cola-new-coke-flopped.

"New Coke: The Most Memorable Marketing Blunder Ever?" https://www.coca-colacompany.com/about-us/history/new-coke-the-most-memorable-marketing-blunder-ever.

Christen, Markus. "Launching New Coke." INSEAD Publishing, January 1, 2001, https://store.hbr.org/product/launching-new-coke/INS982.

Chapter 3: So, What's Your Problem?

Calkins, Tim and Karen White. "Eli Lilly: Xigris (A & B)." Kellogg School of Management, Northwestern University, 2004.

Wilgoren, Jodi. "Jacob Getzels, 89, Educator and Researcher on Creativity," *New York Times,* April 2001.

"The Problem with Making Assumptions," Dr. Sirota blog *(marciasirotamd.com).*

Gladwell, Malcolm. 2004. *Blink: The Power of Thinking Without Thinking.* Boston: Back Bay Books | Hatchett Group.

"How to Define Customer Problems – Part 3 – Identifying Your Riskiest Assumptions." Product Coalition, July 2021.

"The Dangers of Making Assumptions in a Changing World." The Churning, August 2022.

Wedell-Wedellsborg, Thomas. 2020. *What's Your Problem? To Solve Your Toughest Problems, Change the Problems You Solve.* Brighton, Massachusettes:Harvard Business Review Press.

Duhigg, Charles. 2012. *The Power of Habit: Why We Do What We Do in Life and Business.* New York: Random House, pg. 37–43, 52–45.

Damani, Anand. "How the World's Best Marketer Got It Wrong, But Eventually Got It Right." Behavioral Design, June 2016.

Cohan, Peter. *"How P&G Brought Febreze Back to Life,"* Telegram & Gazette, February 2012.

SECTION 2: REFERENCE SOURCES

Chapter 4: Patterns

Hollingworth, Crawford and Liz Barke. "The Behavioural Science Guide to Making and Breaking Habit." (marketingsociety.com), November 2020.

Quinn, J. M. and W. Wood. 2005. *Habits across the Lifespan.* Unpublished manuscript. Raleigh: Duke University.

Wood, W., Quinn, J. M., & Kashy, D., "Habits in everyday life: Thought, emotion, and action." Journal of Personality and Social Psychology, 83, 1281–1297, 2002.

"In the Dark: It took nearly 27 years to solve a notorious child abduction. Why?" Madeleine Baran, APM Reports, December 30, 2016.

"26 years of different leads in Jacob Wetterling's disappearance," FOX 9 Minneapolis-St. Paul (fox9.com), October 30, 2015.

Walters, Julia A., Hanseen, Emily C., Walters, E. Haydn, & Richard Wood-Baker. "Under-diagnosis of chronic obstructive pulmonary disease: A qualitative study in primary care," ScienceDirect, May 2008.

Maykut, P., and Morehouse, R. 1994. *Beginning Qualitative Research: A Philosophic and Practical Guide,* The Falmer Press.

Hill, Kylie, et. al. "Prevalence and underdiagnosis of chronic obstructive pulmonary disease among patients at risk in primary care," Canadian Medical Association Journal, PubMed (nih.gov), April 20, 2010.

"Reduce, Reuse, Recycle . . . Data" 2009 Pharmaceutical Market Research Group (PMRG) Annual National Conference, March 9, 2009.

Chapter 5: Pain Points

Laurie, James. "The Origins of Jobs-to-Be-Done." The Collective Originals, September 2021.

Carmen Nobel. "Clay Christensen's Milkshake Marketing." Harvard Business School Working Knowledge, Feb. 2011.

Krivkovich, Alexis; Liu, Wei Wei; Nguyen Hilary; Rambachan, Ishanaa; Robinson, Nicole; Williams, Monne & Lareina Yee. 2022. *Women in the Workplace,* Charlotte: McKinsey & Company.

Guth, David W. A Simple Guide to Ethnography. (ku.edu), July 23, 2013.

Harper, Christy. "Best practices for ethnographic research, lessons learned in the wild." UX Collective (uxdesign.cc).

Maykut, P. & R. Morehouse. 1994. *Beginning Qualitative Research: A Philosophic and Practical Guide,* Thames Oxfordshire:The Falmer Press.

Sooriyamoorthy, Thushanth & Stephen W. Leslie. "Erectile Dysfunction." National Library of Medicine (NIH). Last updated May 30 2023. (ncbi.nlm.nig.gov).

Elliott, Stuart. Cialis Case: "Viagra and the Battle of Awkward Ads." *New York Times*, April 2004.

Ofek, Elie. "Product Team Cialis—Getting Ready to Market." (Harvard Business School Case 9-505-038) (store.hbr.org), July 2010.

Chapter 6: Perspectives

Kroll, Luisa. "A Fresh Face." *Forbes Magazine*. July 8, 2002.

"The Difference Between Feelings and Emotions," Wake Forest University, September 12, 2019.

Karimova, Hokuma MA. "The Emotion Wheel: What It Is and How to Use It." PositivePsychology.com. 24 December 2017. Scientifically reviewed by Tiffany Sauber Millacci, Ph.D.

Magids, Scott, Zorfas, Alan & Daniel Leemon. "The New Science of Customer Emotions," Harvard Business Review, November 2015.

Dorney, Grace Anne & MA Koppel. "Letter to the Editor: A Patient Perspective." JD, Journal of the COPD Foundation, 2019.

Ansari, Sameera; Hosseinzadeh, Hassan; Dennis, Sarah & Nicholas Zwar. "Patients' perspectives on the impact of a new COPD diagnosis in the face of multimorbidity: a qualitative study." NPJ Primary Care Respiratory Medicine (nature.com), August 14, 2014.

Vozza, Stephanie. "6 Good Ways to Become a Better Listener." March 17, 2017. FastCompany.com.

Novartis touts survival edge in Kisqali's TV debut, Fierce Pharma (fiercepharma.com), March 4, 2020.

Brink, Kyle E. and Robert D. Costigan. "Oral Communication Skills: Are the Priorities of the Workplace and AACSB-Accredited Business Programs Aligned?" Academy of Management Learning & Education (aom.org), March 11, 2015.

Abrahams, Robin and Boris Groysberg. "How to Become a Better Listener." Harvard Business Review (hbr.org), December 21, 2021.

Zenger, Jack and Joseph Folkman. "What Great Listeners Actually Do." Harvard Business Review (hbr.org), July 14, 2016.

Vozza, Stephanie. "6 Good Ways to Become a Better Listener." (fastcompany.com), March 17, 2017.

Schilling, Dianne. "10 Steps to Effective Listening." (forbes.com), November 9, 2012.

Napier-Fitzpatrick, Patricia. "The Lost Art of Listening: 10 Tips for Becoming a Better Listener." Etiquette School of New York (etiquette-ny.com), October 2018.

"Second Time Moms and the Truth About Parenting", The ANA Educational Foundation (aef.com), February 2017.

Chapter 7: Perplexities

Berger, Jonah. (2022) *The Catalyst: How to Change Anyone's Mind.* New York. Simon & Schuster.

Ho, Terence; Cusack, Ruth P.; Chaudhary, Nagendra; Satia, Imran & Om P. Kurmi. "Under- and Over-Diagnosis of COPD: A Global Perspective." PubMed (nih.gov), March 15, 2019.

Hill, Kylie, et. al. "Prevalence and underdiagnosis of chronic obstructive pulmonary disease among patients at risk in primary care," Canadian Medical Association Journal, PubMed (nih.gov), April 20, 2010.

"Chronic Obstructive Pulmonary Disease Public Health Strategic Framework for Prevention," Centers for Disease Control and Prevention. Atlanta, GA (cdc.gov), 2011.

Wheeler, Mark A. "Applying Behavioral Economics to Research Physician Decision-Making." (quirks.com), May 1, 2014.

Menezes, Ana M., et. al. "Continuing to Confront COPD International Surveys: Comparison of patient and physician perceptions about COPD risk and management." International Journal of Chronic Obstructive Pulmonary Disease, PubMed (nih.gov), January 20, 2015.

Carnegie, Dale. 2009. *How to Win Friends and Influence People.* New York: Simon & Schuster, reprint.

Skene, Kiley. "A PR Case Study: Dove Real Beauty Campaign," News Generation (newsgeneration.com), April 11, 2014.

Etcoff, Nancy, MD. "The Real Truth About Beauty: A Global Report, Findings of the Global Study on Women, Beauty and Well-Being." (clubofamsterdam.com) Harvard University, Dr. Susie Orbach, London School of Economics, Dr. Jennifer Scott, StrategyOne, Heidi D'Agostino, StrategyOne, September 2004.

Brooks, Alison Wood and Leslie K. John. "The Surprising Power of Questions." Harvard Business Review (hbr.org), May–June 2018.

"How Smart People Ask Great Questions (and Get Better Answers)." Inc. (inc.com), May 29, 2020.

Ross, Judith. "How to Ask Better Questions." Harvard Business Review (hbr.org), May 6, 2009.

Trident, Mondelēz International, Inc. website, Our Brands, (mondelezinternational.com).

Daniels, Ph.D. Kimberly; Mosher, Ph.D., William D. & Jo Jones, Ph.D. "Contraceptive Methods Women Have Ever Used: United States, 1982–2010." Vital Statistics Division, National Health Statistics Reports, Number 62, February 14, 2015.

Harper, PhD, Cynthia C. et. al. "Evidence-based IUD Practice: Family Physicians and Obstetrician-Gynecologists." PubMed (nih.gov), August 16, 2013.

Gueren, Casey. "This Is the Birth Control Most Doctors Use." Women's Health, (womenshealthmag.com), May 23, 2014.

Thielking, Megan. "When doctors pick their own birth control, IUDs are the most popular option." Vox (vox.com), March 17, 2015.

Stern, Lisa F.; Simons, Hannah R.; Kohn, Julia E.; Debevec, Elie J.; Morfesis, Johanna M. & Ashlesha A. Patel. "Differences in contraceptive use between family planning providers and the U.S. population: results of a nationwide survey." Contraception, February 23, 2015.

Sifferlin, Alexandra. "Why is the most effective form of birth control—the IUD—also the one no one is using?" *Time Magazine*, June 30, 2014.

Black, Kirsten; Lotke, Pamela; Buhling, Kai J. & Nikki B. Zite. "A review of barriers and myths preventing the more widespread use of intrauterine contraception in nulliparous women." *European Journal of Contraception and Reproductive Health Care*, PubMed (nih.gov), October 1, 2012.

"Pros and Cons of Getting Your Tubes Tied," Cool Springs OBGYN (Brentwood, TN) (coolspringsobgyn.com), January 12, 2022.

McNicholas, DO MSCI, Colleen; Madden, MD MPH, Tessa; Secura, PhD, Gina & Jeffrey F. Peipert, MD PhD. "The Contraceptive CHOICE Project Round Up: What we did and what we learned." Clinical Obstetrics Gynecology, PubMed (nih.gov), December 2014.

Daniels, Ph.D., Kimberly and Joyce C. Abma, Ph.D. "Current Contraceptive Status Among Women Aged 15–49: United States, 2017–2019," NCHS Data Brief, Number 288 (cdc.gov), October 2020.

SECTION 3: REFERENCE SOURCES

Chapter 8: Synthesis—Strengthening Your Insight Foundation

"10 best half-marathons across the nations for 2023," *USA Today* 10Best (10best.com), April 7, 2023.

McTigue, K., & Rucker, D. D. (2021) *The Creative Brief Blueprint: Crafting Strategy That Generates More Effective Advertising.* Bookbaby.

"Behavioral Economics: Crash Course Economics #27." Crashcourse | YouTube. March 12, 2016. Video, 10:33:00, https://www.youtube.com/watch?v=dqxQ3E1bubI.

Chapter 9: Becoming an Insight-Based Organization

"Obesity Rises to Top Health Concern for Americans, but Misperceptions Persist." NORC at the University of Chicago, October 2016, accessed August 23, 2023, chrome-extension://efaidnbmnnnibpcajpc glclefindmkaj/https://norc.org/content/dam/norc-org/pdfs/Issue%20 Brief%20A_ASMBS%20NORC%20Obesity%20Poll.pdf.

Marr, Bernard. "The Top 4 Internet of Things Trends in 2023." *Forbes* (via Forbes.com), November 7, 2022.

Van Den Driest, Frank; Sthanunathan, Stan & Keith Weed. "Building and Insights Engine: How Unilever got to know its customers." Harvard Business Review (hbr.org), September 2016.

"Insights2020: Driving Customer-Centric Growth," White Paper, Millward Brown Vermeer, 2015.

Ferrante, J. M.; Piasecki, A. K.; Ohman-Strickland, P. A. & B. F. Crabtree. "Family physicians' practices and attitudes regarding care of extremely obese patients." Obesity (Silver Spring). 2009 Sep;17(9):1710-6. doi: 10.1038/oby.2009.62. Epub 2009 Mar 12. PMID: 19282824; PMCID: PMC2953252.

Final Thoughts

Klein, Gary. 2013. *Seeing What Others Don't: The Remarkable Ways We Gain Insights*. New York: PublicAffairs.

A free ebook edition is available with the purchase of this book.

To claim your free ebook edition:

1. Visit MorganJamesBOGO.com
2. Sign your name CLEARLY in the space
3. Complete the form and submit a photo of the entire copyright page
4. You or your friend can download the ebook to your preferred device

Morgan James
BOGO™

A **FREE** ebook edition is available for you
or a friend with the purchase of this print book.

CLEARLY SIGN YOUR NAME ABOVE

Instructions to claim your free ebook edition:
1. Visit MorganJamesBOGO.com
2. Sign your name CLEARLY in the space above
3. Complete the form and submit a photo of this entire page
4. You or your friend can download the ebook to your preferred device

Print & Digital Together Forever.

Snap a photo

Free ebook

Read anywhere